# Burkina Faso

# WORLD BIBLIOGRAPHICAL SERIES

General Editors:

Robert G. Neville (Executive Editor)

John J. Horton

Robert A. Myers                    Ian Wallace

Hans H. Wellisch        Ralph Lee Woodward, Jr.

**John J. Horton** is Deputy Librarian of the University of Bradford and currently Chairman of its Academic Board of Studies in Social Sciences. He has maintained a longstanding interest in the discipline of area studies and its associated bibliographical problems, with special reference to European Studies. In particular he has published in the field of Icelandic and of Yugoslav studies, including the two relevant volumes in the World Bibliographical Series.

**Robert A. Myers** is Associate Professor of Anthropology in the Division of Social Sciences and Director of Study Abroad Programs at Alfred University, Alfred, New York. He has studied post-colonial island nations of the Caribbean and has spent two years in Nigeria on a Fulbright Lectureship. His interests include international public health, historical anthropology and developing societies. In addition to *Amerindians of the Lesser Antilles: a bibliography* (1981), *A Resource Guide to Dominica, 1493-1986* (1987) and numerous articles, he has compiled the World Bibliographical Series volumes on *Dominica* (1987), *Nigeria* (1989) and *Ghana* (1991).

**Ian Wallace** is Professor of German at the University of Bath. A graduate of Oxford in French and German, he also studied in Tübingen, Heidelberg and Lausanne before taking teaching posts at universities in the USA, Scotland and England. He specializes in contemporary German affairs, especially literature and culture, on which he has published numerous articles and books. In 1979 he founded the journal *GDR Monitor*, which he continues to edit under its new title *German Monitor*.

**Hans H. Wellisch** is Professor emeritus at the College of Library and Information Services, University of Maryland. He was President of the American Society of Indexers and was a member of the International Federation for Documentation. He is the author of numerous articles and several books on indexing and abstracting, and has published *The Conversion of Scripts, Indexing and Abstracting: an International Bibliography* and *Indexing from A to Z*. He also contributes frequently to *Journal of the American Society for Information Science*, *The Indexer* and other professional journals.

**Ralph Lee Woodward, Jr.** is Professor of History at Tulane University, New Orleans. He is the author of *Central America, a Nation Divided*, 2nd ed. (1985), as well as several monographs and more than seventy scholarly articles on modern Latin America. He has also compiled volumes in the World Bibliographical Series on *Belize* (1980), *Nicaragua* (1983), *El Salvador* (1988) and *Guatemala (Rev. Ed.)* (1992). Dr. Woodward edited the Central American section of the *Research Guide to Central America and the Caribbean* (1985) and is currently associate editor of Scribner's *Encyclopedia of Latin American History*.

Please renew/return items by last date
shown. Please call the number below:

Renewals and enquiries:    0300 123 4049

Textphone for hearing or
speech impaired users:    0300 123 4041

www.hertsdirect.org/librarycatalogue
L32

LYMBRIDGE

VOLUME 169

# Burkina Faso

Samuel Decalo

*Compiler*

## CLIO PRESS

OXFORD, ENGLAND · SANTA BARBARA, CALIFORNIA
DENVER, COLORADO

British Library Cataloguing in Publication Data

Burkina Faso. -- (World bibliographical series; vol. 169)
I. Decalo, Samuel    II. Series
016.96625


ISBN 1-85109-214-5


Clio Press Ltd.,
Old Clarendon Ironworks
35A Great Clarendon Street,
Oxford OX2 6AT, England.

ABC-CLIO,
130 Cremona Drive,
Santa Barbara,
CA 93116, USA.


Designed by Bernard Crossland.
Typeset by Columns Design and Production Services Ltd, Reading, England.
Printed and bound in Great Britain by
Bookcraft (Bath) Ltd., Midsomer Norton

# THE WORLD BIBLIOGRAPHICAL SERIES

This series, which is principally designed for the English speaker, will eventually cover every country (and many of the world's principal regions), each in a separate volume comprising annotated entries on works dealing with its history, geography, economy and politics; and with its people, their culture, customs, religion and social organization. Attention will also be paid to current living conditions – housing, education, newspapers, clothing, etc.– that are all too often ignored in standard bibliographies; and to those particular aspects relevant to individual countries. Each volume seeks to achieve, by use of careful selectivity and critical assessment of the literature, an expression of the country and an appreciation of its nature and national aspirations, to guide the reader towards an understanding of its importance. The keynote of the series is to provide, in a uniform format, an interpretation of each country that will express its culture, its place in the world, and the qualities and background that make it unique. The views expressed in individual volumes, however, are not necessarily those of the publisher.

## VOLUMES IN THE SERIES

# Contents

# Contents

# Introduction

Burkina Faso, the successor of Upper Volta, encompasses a territory of 105,870 square miles (274,200 km) and a population of around ten million people. This landlocked country at the centre of West Africa shares borders with six other states: Côte d'Ivoire, Ghana, Togo and Benin in the south, Mali in the north, and Niger in the east. The country is a vast monotonous plateau, drained to the south by the Volta River system. The average height of the plateau is 400 metres above sea level (1,300 feet) with its highest point Mount Nakourou near Mali (749 metres or 2,472 feet). The country receives only 635-1,145 mm of rainfall and has been periodically ravaged by severe droughts. The northern half of the country is relatively arid even in the best of years, although it sustains high population densities, being the centre of the ancient Mossi kingdoms. The country's high population growth and density on poor and progressively degraded soils has given rise to an outward migration of labour to neighbouring Ghana and Côte d'Ivoire (estimated at upwards of 500,000 people a year), which has been the subject of considerable academic research.

The population of Burkina Faso comprises a number of ethnic groups (often divided into the Mossi and Mande peoples), the most numerous of whom are the Mossi (estimated at three million) and the Gourma in the north and east respectively, and the Bobo (350,000) in the southwest. Other sizeable groups include the Fulani (350,000), the Hausa, the nomadic Tuareg with their Bella domestic serfs (250,000) in the northwest, and the Lobi (120,000) in the south.

The vast majority of the population is engaged in subsistence cultivation, mostly living in 7,224 villages, each with an average population of 600. The country's demographic spread is only slowly changing, despite the fact that the capital, Ouagadougou, has doubled its population in just over ten years to 330,000 people, becoming a large urban slum. The country's other urban centres are

**Introduction**

Bobo-Dioulasso (a vibrant economic centre of 175,000), Koudougou (42,000) and Ouahigouya (35,000).

One of the poorest countries in Africa, and in the world, Burkina Faso scores very low on most socio-economic indicators. In the late-1980s illiteracy stood at seventy-eight per cent, with primary school attendance at around twenty-seven per cent. Average life-expectancy is forty-five years, with 14.4% of all children dying before the age of one. Gross national product per capita hovers at around US$330, with a national debt of almost one billion dollars.

Until recently the country's exports were meagre, essentially surpluses of the population's subsistence crops. During the past decade, however, cotton has become Burkina Faso's most important cash crop, as large numbers of farmers have switched, with government encouragement, to production of this more profitable commodity. However, attaining self-sufficiency in basic foodstuffs is the paramount goal in Burkina Faso, in the light of the periodic cycles of droughts which afflict the Sahel region, devastating both cash and subsistence crops.

Formerly governed by France (which conquered the Mossi kingdoms), since independence in 1960 the political history of Upper Volta has been a succession of civilian or military régimes grappling unsuccessfully with the monumental problems posed by the country's abject poverty and ecological constraints. On 4 August 1983, political life took a sudden radical populist lurch when the youthful, charismatic and impetuous Captain Thomas Sankara seized power in a popular coup. A kaleidoscopic series of decrees, programmes, reforms, mobilization drives and nationalizations then followed (including the change in the country's name, to one meaning 'Land of the Incorruptible') as Sankara captured the imagination of people at home and abroad. Many of his actions triggered friction with erstwhile allies (France) and neighbouring states (Mali, Côte d'Ivoire) while the reforms caused unrest among both the largely conservative rural Mossi and the always powerful trade unions. More importantly, Sankara's highly impetuous and individualistic leadership style ultimately drove a wedge between him and his former colleagues in the military.

The Sankara era ended on 15 October 1987 when his close companion, Captain Blaise Campaore, seized power (with Sankara dying in a bloody confrontation) to announce a 'democratic rectification' of the 1983 Revolution. Shortly afterwards, the government became subject to global pressures for the democratization of Africa to which Campaore had to accede, ushering in competitive elections in which he was confirmed as Head of State.

The literature on Burkina Faso poses three sets of problems for the reader who seeks further knowledge about the country: language, access and an uneven spread of the literature. The first problem relates to the fact that the vast bulk of the literature on all aspects of Burkina Faso is in French. Although scattered exceptions exist, only in four fields can interested readers find adequate or ample material in English: on Mossi history, largely due to the prolific work of one scholar, Elliott Percival Skinner; on labour migration and grain-marketing issues, where Myron Joel Echenberg has conducted seminal research; on current events, where there is actually an abundance of annuals, monthly research tools, and individual articles; and on travel and tourism.

The second problem concerns the difficulty of accessing the literature on Burkina Faso, whether in English or in French. While any large university library (and some public libraries) is likely to carry the basic research staples (such as *Africa Contemporary Record*; *Africa South of the Sahara*; *Africa Research Bulletin*) which provide concise overviews of developments in all African states, their other holdings of literature on Burkina Faso, especially that in French, is often very modest. By far the most impressive and concentrated collection of material (in any language) in the United States is found in the Library of Congress, whose holdings include many titles difficult to trace in Paris itself. Such research should be comple-mented by a visit to the venerable New York Public Library which often seems to possess precisely what is missing in Washington. As to the UK, although I cannot speak with the same degree of certitude about British libraries, I have always been especially impressed with the holdings of the library of the London School of Oriental and African Studies which contains more than meets the eye at first glance, though research amenities are less developed than those in the United States.

The problem of access is paradoxically also true in France where even outstanding libraries often have a dearth of material (in French-language sources) where Burkina Faso is concerned. Serious research would ideally require work in several centres, commencing with the Documentation Française library in Paris (whose hours have been cut for reasons of economy), and continuing with the collections at the Sorbonne and CEAN at the University of Bordeaux. In Paris, the cavernous retail outlet of Harmattan (on Rue des Ecoles near the Sorbonne) is invaluable, and although a major publisher of Africana, it also stocks copies of (often long out-of-print) titles from other publishers, and conducts title searches and purchases on behalf of customers.

Finally, there is the problem of the uneven spread of the literature on Burkina Faso. Certain subjects have attracted an inordinate

**Introduction**

amount of attention, often from a handful of very productive
scholars, while on other themes the literature is very sparse indeed.
These disparities are consequently reflected in this bibliography,
which mirrors existing research preoccupations. The study of the
ethnology and history of Burkina Faso, for example, has always been
a magnet for French scholarship, but until fairly recently much of this
research has been highly selective, dealing largely with the Mossi,
whose ancient kingdoms (especially Yatenga) have attracted enor-
mous attention, to the exclusion of other groups and their histories.
This volume attempts to guide those who have an interest in this
fascinating, if impoverished, country through the major body of
literature that exists, especially that in the English language.

*Samuel Decalo*
*University of Florida*
*November 1993*

# Theses and Dissertations on Burkina Faso

Donald M. Austin. 'Heat stress and heat tolerance in two African populations', PhD thesis, Pennsylvania State University, 1974, 142p.

Amadé Badini. 'Système éducatif moaga, Burkina Faso, et action éducative scolaire; essai d'une pédagogie de l'oralité' (The Moaga, Burkina Faso, educational system and school education action: essay on the pedagogics of orality), PhD thesis, Lille University, 1990, 658p.

Elvira Beckett. 'A linguistic analysis of Gurma', MA thesis, University of British Columbia, 1974, 151p.

J. Bécuwé. 'Eléments de phonologie et de grammaire du Lobiri' (Elements of the phonology and grammar of Lobiri), PhD thesis, University of Paris, 1982, 479p.

Diarra Sadek Boubacar. 'Political change, rural transformation and development administration: the politics of change and development in Francophone Africa with special reference to the Upper Volta', PhD thesis, University of Minnesota, 1974, 275p.

Herbert W. Butter. 'The structuring process in a Mossi village', PhD thesis, Michigan State University, 1975, 312p.

Garry Neil Christensen. 'Determinants of private investment in rural Burkina Faso', PhD thesis, Cornell University, 1989, 254p.

L. Coulibaly. 'L'Autorité dans l'Afrique traditionnelle: l'étude comparative des états Mossi en Graudo' (Authority in traditional Africa: a comparative study of the Mossi states in Graudo), PhD thesis, Laval University, 1972, 289p.

Sidiki Coulibaly. 'Les migrations Voltaiques, les origines, les motifs et les perceptions des politiques' (Voltaic migrations, origins, purpose and the views of the politicians), PhD thesis, Montreal University, 1979, 795p.

Sidiki Philippe Coulibaly. 'Socio-cultural values and fertility: the case of Upper Volta', MA thesis, Cornell University, 1972, 98p.

Christopher Linn Delgado. 'Livestock versus food grain production in southeastern Upper Volta: a resource allocation analysis', PhD thesis, Cornell University, 1978, 443p.

H. Pamateba Diendere. 'Analysis of supply and demand of millet and sorghum in Upper Volta', MSc thesis, Michigan State University, 1984, 123p.

Myron Joel Echenberg. 'African reaction to French conquest: Upper Volta in the late nineteenth century', PhD thesis, University of Wisconsin, 1971, 337p.

Lynn Ellsworth. 'Mutual insurance and non-market transactions among farmers in Burkina Faso', PhD thesis, University of Wisconsin, 1988, 343p.

Marcel Fafchamps. 'Sequential decisions under uncertainty and labor market failure: a model of household behavior in the African semi-arid tropics (Burkina Faso)', PhD thesis, University of California at Berkeley, 1989, 359p.

Gregory F. Finnegan. 'Population movement, labor, migration, and social structure in a Mossi village', PhD thesis, Brandeis University, 1976, 274p.

Allan Page Fisk. 'Making up society: four models for constructing social relations among the Moose of Burkina Faso', PhD thesis, University of Chicago, 1985, 277p.

Robert Elden Ford. 'Subsistence farming systems in semi-arid northern Yatenga', PhD thesis, University of California at Riverside, 1982, 674p.

Pascal Tagne Fotzo. 'The economics of *bas-fond* rice production in the eastern region of Upper Volta: a whole farm approach,' PhD thesis, Michigan State University, 1983, 273p.

Anne Elizabeth Garber. 'A tonal analysis of Senufo: Sucite dialect', PhD thesis, University of Illinois at Urbana-Champaign, 1987, 412p.

Myriam Gervais. 'Capital transnational, capital national, état et paysans au Mali et au Burkina Faso: les projets cotonniers mali-sud et ouest-volta 1976–1987' (Transnational capital, national capital, state and rural communities in South Mali and West Volta 1976–1987), PhD thesis, Quebec University, 1989, 278p.

Eren Giray-Laul. 'Jula oral narratives in Bobo Dioulasso: continuity, recreation, and transcultural communication', PhD thesis, Indiana University, 1989, 310p.

Joel Wayne Gregory. 'Underdevelopment, dependency, and migration in Upper Volta', PhD thesis, Cornell University, 1974, 331p.

Mouhamadou Gueye. 'Birth weight and body weight: correlates and association with morbidity and mortality in Bobo Dioulasso', PhD thesis, University of Pennsylvania, 1987, 232p.

Peter B. Hammond. 'Technological change and Mossi acculturation', PhD thesis, Northwestern University, 1962, 216p.

Robert Douglas Hardy. 'Education and economic development in the Upper Volta', PhD thesis, University of Michigan, 1978, 138p.

Grace Salome Hemmings-Gapihan. 'Women and economy in Gourma, 1919–1978', PhD thesis, Yale University, 1985, 389p.

Larry Allen Herman. 'The livestock and meat-marketing system in Upper Volta: an evaluation of economic efficiency', PhD thesis, University of Michigan, 1981, 436p.

Pierre Ilboudou. 'Contribution à l'histoire religieuse du peuple Mossi de Haute-Volta' (Contribution to the religious history of the Mossi in Upper Volta), PhD thesis, University of Paris, 1970, 323p.

Joseph Paul Irwin. 'An emirate of the Niger Bend: A political history of Liptako in the nineteenth century', PhD thesis, University of Wisconsin, 1973, 208p.

Michel Izard. 'Les archives orales d'un royaume africain. Recherche sur la formation du Yatenga' (The oral archives of an African kingdom. Research into the development of Yatenga), PhD thesis, University of Paris, 1980, 421p.

William Kenneth Jaeger. 'Agricultural mechanization: the economics of animal traction in Burkina Faso', PhD thesis, Stanford University, 1985, 261p.

Charles Kabéya Muasé. 'Syndicalisme et structuration du champ politique au Burkina Faso' (Trade unionism and the structuring of the political arena in Burkina Faso), PhD thesis, Institut Catholique de Paris, 1988, 681p.

Michel Kabore. 'Syntactic transfer in third language learning: pedagogical implications', PhD thesis, University of Texas at Austin, 1983, 172p.

Wilma Ardine Lyghtner Kirchhofer. 'Nutrient analyses of uncultivated vegetation from Burkina Faso, West Africa', PhD thesis, University of Missouri-Columbia, 1986, 132p.

Gregory Charles Lassiter. 'The impact of animal traction on farming systems in eastern Upper Volta', PhD thesis, Cornell University, 1982, 291p.

Della Elizabeth McMillan. 'A resettlement project in Upper Volta', PhD thesis, Northwestern University, 1983, 448p.

James Daniel McNiven. 'French aid policies toward the African territories: from Empire to Independence', PhD thesis, University of Michigan, 1972, 365p.

Brenda Gael McSweeney. 'The negative impact of development on women reconsidered: a study of the Women's Education Project in Upper Volta', PhD thesis, Tufts University, 1979, 278p.

J. Y. Marchal. 'Société, espace et désertification dans le Yatenga, ou la dynamique de l'espace rural soudano-sahélien' (Society, space and the population drain in Yatenga, or the dynamics of the Sudano-Sahelian rural areas), PhD thesis, University of Paris, 1983, 540p.

Kathryn F. Mason. 'A woman's place: the articultation of social structure by Moose co-wives and mothers, Burkina Faso', PhD thesis, University of Chicago, 330p.

Cheikh Seydi Moctar Mbacke. 'Estimating child mortality from retrospective reports by mothers at time of a new birth: the case of the EMIS surveys', PhD thesis, University of Pennsylvania, 1986, 181p.

T. Melegue. 'La variable militaire dans la politique africaine de la Haute-Volta 1966–1978', (The military variable in the African policies of Upper Volta 1966–1978), PhD thesis, University of Bordeaux, 1981, 406p.

Joy Florence Morrison. 'Communications and social change: a case study of forum theater in Burkina Faso', PhD thesis, University of Iowa, 1991, 209p.

Mary Lynn Alice Morse. 'A sketch of the phonology and morphology of Bobo', PhD thesis, Columbia University, 1976, 203p.

Kifle Negash. 'An assessment of the integrated rural development program in eastern Upper Volta', PhD thesis, Michigan State University, 1983, 323p.

A. Nikiéma. 'Evolution du régime politique de la Haute-Volta depuis l'indépendence' (The evolution of the political régime of Upper Volta since independence), PhD thesis, University of Poitiers, 1979, 467p.

Norbert Nikiéma. 'On the linguistic bases of Moore orthography,' PhD thesis, Indiana University, 1976, 239p.

Ismael S. Ouedraogo. 'A socio-economic analysis of farmers' food grain marketing linkages in eastern Upper Volta', PhD thesis, Michigan State University, 1983, 321p.

F. O. Pale 'Connaissance du milieu et développement rural au sud-ouest de la Haute-Volta: les problèmes d'intégration du paysan lobi dans l'agriculture moderne' (Knowledge of the area and rural development in southwest Upper Volta: the problems of integrating rural Lobi into modern agriculture), PhD thesis, University of Strasbourg, 1980, 208p.

Ginette Pallier. 'Géographie générale de la Haute-Volta' (General geography of Upper Volta), PhD thesis, University of Limoges, 1978, 241p.

M. Pere. 'Les deux bouches. Les sociétés du "rameau lobi" entre la tradition et le changement' (The two mouths. The 'Lobi branch' societies between tradition and change), PhD thesis, University of Paris, 1982, 296p.

Jean-Vlaude Pion. 'Alteration des massifs cristallins basiques en zone tropicale sèche: étude de quelques toposéquences en Haute-Volta' (Weathering of the basic crystalline massifs in a dry tropical zone: a study of a few toposequences in Upper Volta), PhD thesis, University of Strasbourg, 1979, 220p.

Yves Coffi Prudencio. 'A village study of soil fertility management and food crop production in Upper Volta: Technical and economic analysis', PhD thesis, University of Arizona, 1983, 388p.

Lucy Gardner Quimby. 'Transformations of belief: Islam among the Dyula of Kongbougou', PhD thesis, University of Wisconsin, 1972, 250p.

Sunder Ramaswamy. 'Technological change, land use patterns and household income distribution in the Sahel: the Burkina Faso example', PhD thesis, Purdue University, 1991, 173p.

Paula Donnelly Roark. 'Authentic education and development: West African perspectives from Upper Volta', PhD thesis, University of Colorado at Boulder, 1979, 214p.

John Michael Roth. 'Economic evaluation of agricultural policy in Burkina Faso: a social modelling approach', PhD thesis, Purdue University, 1986, 533p.

Christopher Damon Roy. 'Mossi masks and crests', PhD thesis, Indiana University, 1979, 1979p.

Fenton Bracid Sands. 'An economic analysis of farm level livestock marketing in eastern Upper Volta', PhD thesis, Michigan State University, 1984, 264p.

Fernand Sanou. 'African universities in search of their identity: a study of the culture of careerism at the University of Ouagadougou', PhD thesis, University of Southern California, 1982, 383p.

Saidou Sanou. 'Land tenure structures in the agricultural sector of Hounde, Burkina Faso: study in rural social change and development', PhD thesis, Michigan State University, 1986, 197p.

Mahir Saul. 'Stratification and leveling in the farming economy of a Voltaic village', PhD thesis, Indiana University, 1982, 336p.

Kimseyinga Savadogo. 'An analysis of the economic and socio-demographic determinants of household food consumption in Ouagadougou', PhD thesis, Purdue University, 1986, 213p.

Geremie Sawadogo. 'A policy analysis of the language reform in

Burkina Faso from 1979 to 1984', PhD thesis, University of Iowa, 1990, 260p.

Jacqueline Ruth Sherman. 'Grain markets and the marketing behavior of farmers: a case study of Manga, Upper Volta', PhD thesis, University of Michigan, 1984, 366p.

Stuart David Showalter. 'Surveying sociolinguistic aspects of interethnic contact in rural Burkina Faso', Georgetown University, 1991, 404p.

C. Some. 'Sociologie du pouvoir militaire: le cas de la Haute-Volta' (The sociology of military power: the case of Upper Volta), PhD thesis, University of Bordeaux, 1979, 325p.

Frederick Walter Sowers. 'Moving on: Migration and agropastoral production among the Fulbe in southern Burkina Faso', PhD thesis, University of California at Berkeley, 1986, 368p.

Richard Swanson. 'Gourma ethnoanatomy: a theory of human being', PhD thesis, Northwestern University, 1976, 455p.

Ellen Jean Szarleta. 'An economic analysis of the sociomarket and market economies: a case study of Burkina Faso', PhD thesis, University of Wisconsin, 1987, 281p.

Edouard Kouka Tapsoba. 'An economic and institutional analysis of formal and informal credit in eastern Upper Volta: empirical evidence and policy implications', PhD thesis, Michigan State University, 1981, 309p.

Tisna Patricia Veldhuyzen Van Zanten. 'Migration and household reproduction: a study among the Bissa of Burkina Faso', PhD thesis, University of California, Berkeley, 1986, 307p.

Bassey Eteyen Wai-Ogosu. 'Archaeological reconnaisance of Upper Volta', PhD thesis, University of California Berkeley, 1973, 189p.

# The Country and Its People

1 **Atlas de la Haute-Volta.** (Atlas of Upper Volta.)
Paris: Editions Jeune-Afrique, 1975. 48p. maps.
A series of concise articles, each illustrated by colour maps, covering a wide variety of
subjects concerning Upper Volta, including geography, geology, climate, vegetation,
soil, ethnic groups, demographic spread, cities, urbanization, communications,
agriculture, industry, education, and health. That is followed by a region-by-region
overview, also accompanied by maps. One of Jeune-Afrique's earlier surveys of
African states, the work is dated in some respects, but has not been surpassed as a
compact and graphic portrayal of all aspects of the country.

2 **Burkina Faso.**
Ralph Uwechue (et al.). In: *Know Africa: Africa today.* London:
Africa Books, 1991. 2nd ed., p. 587-615. map.
A comprehensive compendium of historical, economic and political information. The
chapter is especially useful on post-1960 events, developments since President
Sankara's assassination, and on the Burkinabe economy. The chapter concludes with
sixteen tables, and lists of the 1991 government and Burkinabe diplomatic missions
abroad.

3 **Burkina Faso.**
Sean Moroney. In: *Africa.* New York: Facts on File, 1989, vol. 1,
p. 45-58.
The author provides an overview of all aspects of Burkina Faso, covering its
geography, peoples, economy, constitution, political parties, and recent social, political
and economic history.

1

## The Country and Its People

4 **Burkina Faso.**
Aaron Lear. Edgemont, Pennsylvania: Chelsea House, 1986. 95p. maps.

A colourfully illustrated introduction to the topography, people and culture of Burkina Faso, with particular emphasis on the economy, industry and the country's rôle in the world.

5 **Haut-Sénégal–Niger. Le pays, les peuples, les langues, l'histoire, les civilisations.** (Upper Senegal–Niger. The country, the people, the languages, the history, the civilizations.)
Maurice Delafosse. Paris: Maisonneuve et Larose, 1972. 3 vols. maps. bibliog.

This is a reprint of the 1912 classic encyclopaedic study of the French colony of Haut-Senegal–Niger, part of which was to become Upper Volta. Delafosse was an historian, ethnographer, linguist and colonial administrator, who is honoured throughout France in the names of streets, schools and buildings. A prolific author, this study won Delafosse an award from the Académie Française. The work is organized into five parts: the country; the peoples; languages; history; and the civilizations which sprang up in the area. A seventy-seven-page index provides reference to material relevant to the Mossi and Burkina Faso in general. As with other early works, Delafosse is inclined to accept oral history uncritically, including, for example, the supposed Jewish origins of the Fulani.

6 **Upper Volta.**
John Allan, Janice E. Baker. Chicago, Illinois: Children's Press, 1974, 96p.

A children's book, profusely illustrated with black-and-white photographs, providing an introduction to the geography, people, history, resources, cities and evolution of Upper Volta.

2

# Geography and Geology

7 **Atlas des villages de Haute-Volta.** (Atlas of Upper Volta's villages.)
Institut National de la Statistique et de la Démographie. Ouagadougou:
Ministère du Plan et de la Coopération, 1982. [n.p.]. maps.
The official atlas of Burkina Faso's 1975 census districts and their villages. It
comprises a total of fifty-two maps on a scale of 1:200,000.

8 **Le bassin du fleuve Volta.** (The Volta river basin.)
F. Moniod, B. Pouyaud, P. Sechet.   Paris: ORSTOM, 1977. 513p. maps.
bibliog.
A comprehensive hydrological study which considers the Volta river basin, an area of
395,000 square kilometres. The work covers climatic conditions, waterflow measurements on the two Volta rivers and their tributaries, and seasonal variations.

9 **Contribution a l'évaluation de l'évaporation de nappes d'eau libre en
climat tropical sec.** (Contribution to the assessment of evaporation of
open expanses of water in a dry tropical climate.)
B. Pouyaud.   Paris: ORSTOM, 1986. 254p. maps. bibliog.
A three-country meteorological/water evaporation study of arid regions.

10 **Essai sur l'écologie et la sociologie d'arbres et arbustes de Haute Volta.**
(Essay on the sociology and ecology of trees and shrubs in Upper Volta.)
M. Terrible.   Bobo-Dioulasso, Burkina Faso: Librairie de la Savane,
1984. 254p. maps. bibliog.
Written by a well-known priest, this study is a comprehensive survey of Burkina Faso's
terrain including topics such as soils, rainfall patterns, humidity, geographical
substrata, population density, soil degradation and desertification patterns. The work is
profusely illustrated with maps, tables and diagrams, and concludes with an extensive
bibliography.

3

## Geography and Geology

11 **Etat des connaissances hydrogéologiques en Haute Volta.** (State of hydrological knowledge in Upper Volta.)
C. Diluca. Ouagadougou: Comité Interafricaine d'Etudes Hydrauliques, 1979. 75p. map.

Inventory of existing underground water resources and needs of Burkina Faso, and the sources of this data. See also E. Roose and J. Piot, 'Runoff, erosion and soil fertility restoration on the Mossi plateau', in *Challenges in African hydrology and water resources*, edited by D. E. Walling (et al.) (Oxford: International Association of Hydrological Sciences, 1984, p. 485-98).

12 **Etude géologique et structurale du nord-ouest Dahomey, du nord Togo et du sud-est Haute-Volta.** (Geological study of northwest Dahomey, north Togo and southeast Upper Volta.)
Pascal Affaton. Marseille: Laboratoire des Sciences de la Terre, 1975. 203p. maps. bibliog.

A detailed geological survey of southeastern Burkina Faso, published as part of a regional study which also covers north Benin and Togo.

13 **Géographie générale de la Haute Volta.** (General geography of Upper Volta.)
Ginette Pallier. Limoges, France: Université de Limoges, 1978. 241p. maps.

Pallier's work is the standard physical and social geography of Burkina Faso.

14 **Gold in Birrimian greenstone belts of Burkina Faso.**
Daniel Huot (et al.). *Economic Geology*, vol. 82, no. 8 (1987), p. 2033-44. maps. bibliog.

A geological study of the prevalence and levels of concentration of gold deposits found in Burkina Faso's greenstone belts. Many such deposits are known to exist in the country, some of which were mined in pre-colonial days.

15 **Le potentiel minier de la république de Haute-Volta.** (Mineral potential of the republic of Upper Volta.)
Jean Marcelin. Ouagadougou: Ministère du Commerce, du Développement Industriel et des Mines, 1975, 241p. maps. bibliog.

Geological survey of Burkina Faso and inventory of the country's mineral deposits. The study lists all sites where exploratory work or mining has already been conducted, and specifies what infrastructure would be needed to bring on stream all known deposits. For a more recent report on mineral explorations, see J. Kabore, 'Prospection géochimique dans le centre et nord-centre du Burkina Faso' (Geochemical prospecting in the central and north-central Burkina Faso), *Journal of Geochemical Exploration* (New York), vol. 32, no. 1-3 (1989), p. 429-35.

16  **Proposition pour une géographie des climats en Côte-d'Ivoire et au Burkina Faso.** (A suggestion for a climatological geography of the Ivory Coast and Burkina Faso.)
Gerard Riou.  In: *Le climat de la savane de Lamto (Côte d'Ivoire) et sa place dans les climats de l'Ouest Africain* (The climate of the Lamto Savana (Ivory Coast) and its place in the climates of West Africa), edited by Maxime Lamont, Jean-Louis Tierford.  Paris: Ecole Normale Supérieure, 1989. p. 81-115. bibliog.
A climatological study of the Ivory Coast and Burkina Faso with detailed monthly temperatures, rainfall tables and air circulation charts.

17  **Soil physical properties of tied ridges in the Sudan savannah of Burkina Faso.**
N. R. Hulugalle, M. S. Rodriguez.  *Experimental Agriculture*, vol. 24, no. 3 (July 1988), p. 375-91. bibliog.
The physical properties of the soils of the tied ridges in Burkina Faso are examined in this article. Measurements in 1983 indicated that these were most affected by the type of seed-bed and clay content. The article is complemented by N. R. Hulugalle (et al.), 'Effect of rock bunds and tied ridges on soil water content and soil properties in the Sudan savannah of Burkina Faso', *Tropical Agriculture*, vol. 67, no. 2 (June 1990), p. 149-53.

18  **Sols et problèmes de fertilité en Haute Volta.** (Problems of soil fertility in Upper Volta.)
J. J. Jenny.  *Agronomie Tropicale* (Paris) (Feb. 1965), p. 220-47. map.
Jenny's account of the country's geological and climatic conditions is followed by a description of the principal types of soil. Since most of the latter are of poor quality, procedures needed to enrich them and increase agrarian productivity are outlined. There is an English summary of the article.

19  **The Tambao manganese mines.**
Jacques J. Boulanger.  *Entente Africaine* (Paris), (July 1969), p. 68-74.
A description of the huge and inaccessible manganese deposits in southwest Burkina Faso, the exploitation of which the government hopes will assist in transforming the country.

20  **Toposéquences de sols tropicaux en Haute-Volta: équilibre et déséquilibre bioclimatique.** (Toposequences of tropical soils in Upper Volta. Equilibrium and bioclimatic disequilibrium.)
René Boulet.  Paris: ORSTOM, 1978. 272p. bibliog.
Parts of Burkina Faso's soils are unstable, and subject to transformation to montmorillonite plasma in dynamic equilibrium with the pedoclimatic conditions in their zones. This book provides an account of the problems of soils in Burkina Faso, with a summary in English.

21 **Upper Volta: Official Standard Names Approved by the United States Board on Geographic Names.**
Washington, DC: Government Printing Office, 1965. 168p.
A directory of officially designated geographical names for Burkina Faso cartography.

22 **Yatenga nord Haute-Volta, la dynamique d'un espace rural soudano-sahelien.** (Upper Volta's northern Yatenga, the dynamics of a Sudano-sahelian region.)
Yves J. Marchal. Paris: ORSTOM, 1983. 873p. maps.
Marchal's work constitutes a massive contribution to the geography of northern Yatenga. In 1975 the region had a population of 123,000 (seventy per cent of them farmers) and a population density of seventy-two per square kilometre, nearly double the population density of the rest of Yatenga. Apart from the capital, Ouahigouya, the region is rural, and much of the land has only poor or medium-quality soils. The work describes climate, drought, vegetation and human habitation patterns.

**Atlas de la Haute-Volta.** (Atlas of Upper Volta.)
*See* item no. 1.

# Flora and Fauna

23 **La flore forestière de Haute Volta.** (The forest flora of Upper Volta.)
J. Tiquet. *Etudes Scientifiques* (Paris), (Sept.-Dec. 1983). 43p.
This special issue is a profusely illustrated alphabetical compendium of sixty-four
varieties of forest flora found in Burkina Faso. There are some 200 other species, but
their prevalence and utility is marginal.

24 **Lexique commenté peul–latin des flores de Haute Volta.** (Fulani–Latin
annotated list of Upper Volta flora.)
Danièle Klintz, Bernard Toutain. Maison-Alfort, France: Institut
d'Elevage et de Médicine Vétérinaire des Pays Tropicaux, 1981. 44p.
(Etude botanique, no. 10).
Annotated and illustrated compendium, with Fulani names and their Latin counter-
parts, of Burkina Faso's flora.

25 **Les mantes du Burkina Faso.** (The mantises of Burkina Faso.)
A. Prost, R. Roy. *Bulletin d'IFAN* (Dakar), vol. 45, no. 1/2 (1983),
p. 1114-26.
Description of Burkina Faso's mantises. For some notes on the presence of rodent
species in Burkina Faso, see B. Sicard (et al.), 'Un Rongeur nouveau du Burkina Faso'
(A new rodent in Burkina Faso), *Mammalia*, vol. 52, no. 2 (1988), p. 187-98.

## Flora and Fauna

26 **Petit atlas de classification, de morphologie, de répartition et de détermination des animaux sauvages de Haute-Volta.** (Small atlas on the classification, morphology and distribution of wild animals in Burkina Faso.)
Georges Roure. Ouagadougou: Haute-Volta Direction des Eaux et des Forêts, 1968. 31p.
The atlas contains illustrated tabulation and classification of all wild animals found in Burkina Faso.

27 **Les plantes en pays Lobi.** (Plants in Lobi country.)
Odile Hoffman. Maison-Alfort, France: Institut d'Elevage et de Médicine Vétérinaire, 1987. 155p. map.
Ethnobotanical study and dictionary enumerating all plants found in Lobi regions, with their indigenous and Latin names.

28 **Les poissons des hauts bassins de la Volta.** (The fish of the upper reaches of the Volta.)
Roman Benigno. Tervuren, Belgium: Musée Royal de l'Afrique Centrale, 191p. maps. bibliog.
Of the 300 species of fish in the four branches of the Volta river basin, 114 are catalogued, described, and illustrated in this book.

# Prehistory and Archaeology

29 **Archéologie et tradition orale: contribution à l'histoire des espaces du pays d'Aribinda.** (Archaeology and oral tradition: a contribution to the history of the Aribinda area.)
Georges Dupré, Dominique Guilland. *Cahiers des Sciences Humaines* (Paris), vol. 22, no. 1 (1986), p. 5-48. bibliog.

Based on oral tradition, archaeological remains and cave-drawings, several hypotheses are presented concerning the ancient populations of the province of Soum. The author expands on earlier research reported in Jean Rouch (et al.), 'Restes anciens et gravures rupestres d'Aribinda' (Ancient remains and rupestrian engravings in Aribinda), *Etudes Voltaïques* (Ouagadougou), no. 2 (1963), p. 61-70. An English summary is included.

30 **Carte et répertoire des sites néolithiques du Mali et de la Haute Volta.** (Map and inventory of Neolithic sites in Mali and Upper Volta.)
Raymond Guitat. *Bulletin d'IFAN* (Dakar), vol. 34, no. 4 (1972), p. 896-925. map.

An inventory of various Neolithic sites discovered in Upper Volta and in neighbouring Mali.

31 **Frühistorische Bodenfunde im Raum von Mengao.** (Prehistoric excavation findings in the Mengao region.)
Annemarie Schweeger-Hefel. Vienna: H. Bohlaus, 1965. 71p. map.

A study based on the excavation of tombs in the Mengao region in the early 1960s. For another article by this prolific author see 'Zur Frage megalithischer Elemente bei den Kurumba' (On the question of megalithic elements of the Kurumba), *Zeitschrift für Ethnologie* (Braunschweig), vol. 88, no. 2 (1963), p. 266-92. See also Bassey Andah, 'Excavations at Rim, north-central Upper Volta' in *West African Cultural Dynamics* edited by B. K. Swartz, R. E. Dumett (The Hague: Mouton, 1980, p. 41-65. map).

## Prehistory and Archaeology

32 **L'or de la Volta Noire. Archéologie et histoire de l'exploitation traditionnelle.** (The gold of the Black Volta: archaeology and history of traditional exploitation.)
Jean-Baptiste Kiethega. Paris: Karthala, 1983. 247p. maps. bibliog.
Combining oral tradition and archaeological evidence, the author pieces together the history of gold exploitation in the Poura region of the Gurunsi of Burkina Faso from the seventeenth century to 1965, when the last French mine closed down. Specific sites of ancient digs are identified, as well as the manner of exploitation and the rôle of gold in society and its markets.

33 **Prehistoric reconnaissance of parts of North Central Upper Volta: its bearing on agricultural beginnings.**
Bassey W. Andah. *Bulletin d'IFAN* (Dakar). vol. 42, no. 2 (April 1980), p. 219-50. maps.
This comprehensive outline of the origins and nature of agriculture in North Central Burkina Faso is based on palaeoanthropological and archaeological research. The author expanded his scope in a later article, 'Prehistoric reconnaissance of North Eastern parts of Upper Volta', *West African Journal of Archaeology* (Ibadan), vol. 12 (1982), p. 82-93. map.

34 **Vestiges préhistoriques en pays Bobo.** (Prehistoric remains in Bobo country.)
Guy Le Moal. *Cahiers d'ORSTOM* (Paris), vol. 78, no. 2 (1981/2), p. 255-60.
A brief inventory and review of prehistoric settlement sites in regions inhabited by the Bobo of Burkina Faso. The author is a noted anthropologist.

# History

## Colonial conquest and rule

35 **L'échec d'une conquête: le pays lobi (1900-1926).** (The failure of a
conquest: Lobi country.)
Danielle Domergue. *Bulletin de l'IFAN* (Dakar), vol. 39, no. 3 (1977),
p. 532-53. map.

The history of the Lobi, a people who are divided by international borders and inhabit
three states, is still not fully known. The author surveys the French penetration of Lobi
areas, the imposition of colonial rule, and the rôle of Labouret in shaping policy vis-à-
vis the Lobi. For an article on the the period just prior to the subjugation of the Lobi
see Daniel Dory, 'Entre la découverte et la domination: les Lobi' (Between discovery
and domination: the Lobi), *Bulletin de l'Association de Géographie* (Paris), vol. 61, no.
505/6 (1984), p. 373-82.

36 **Esquisse de la conquête et de la formation territoriale de la colonie de
Haute-Volta.** (Survey of the conquest and territorial shaping of the
colony of Upper Volta.)
Georges Y. Madiega. *Bulletin de l'IFAN* (Dakar). vol. 43 no. 3/4
(1981), p. 218-77. maps. bibliog.

Comprehensive survey of the Mossi and Gurma kingdoms, Fulani emirates and
Gurunsi groups on the eve of the French military occupation. The author, who
teaches history at the University of Ouagadougou, also outlines the administrative
organization of the conquered areas. Madiega has also written a study of the
precolonial history of the Gurma: *Contribution à l'histoire précoloniale du Gulma*
(Contribution to the precolonial history of Gulma) (Wiesbaden, Germany: F. Steiner,
1982. 260p.). For an account of some of the revolts which erupted after the French
occupation, see Jean Hebert, 'Révoltes en Haute-Volta de 1914 à 1918' (Revolts in
Upper Volta from 1914 to 1918), *Notes et Documents Voltaïques* (Ouagadougou), vol.
3, no. 4 (July 1970), p. 3-55; and Blami Gnakambary 'La révolte bobo de 1916 dans le

11

cercle de Dedougou' (The Bobo revolt of 1916 in the Dedougou circle), *Notes et Documents Voltaïques* (Ouagadougou), vol. 3, no. 4 (July 1970), p. 55-87.

37 **Evolution de la Haute Volta de 1898 au 3 janvier 1966.** (Evolution of Upper Volta from 1898 to 3 January 1966.)
François Djoby Bassolet. Ouagadougou: Imprimerie Nationale, 1968. 135p. map.

Written from a Burkinabe perspective, this book is a compact history of the country from its conquest by the French until the fall of the First Republic of President Maurice Yaméogo. Photographs of the main historical figures, and texts of various speeches and proclamations are included. Events leading to the 1966 coup d'état are detailed on a day-to-day basis, and for 3 January on an hourly basis. This is a valuable work as some of the material in the book is difficult to obtain from other sources.

38 **Genèse de la Haute-Volta.** (Origins of Upper Volta.)
Salfo Albert Balima. Ouagadougou: Presses Africaines, 1969. 253p.

Written by a Burkinabe scholar and international administrator, the work briefly surveys the pre-colonial context, the French conquest, and the policies and consequences of French rule. The work is interspersed with photographs of the royal court of Tenkodogo and contains a 105-page addenda of documents, historic letters, statutes of the early political parties and lists of Voltaic representatives to colonial structures, the latter difficult to locate elsewhere.

39 **Les Gourounsi de Haute-Volta: conquête et colonisation, 1896-1933.** (The Gurunsi of Upper Volta: conquest and colonization, 1896-1933.)
A. M. Duperray. Stuttgart, Germany: F. Steiner, 1984. 280p. bibliog.

This is a comprehensive study of initial French contacts with the Gurunsi, their subjugation, and the early colonial policies affecting them.

40 **Jihad and state-building in late nineteenth century Upper Volta: the rise and fall of the state of Al-Kari of Bousse.**
Myron Joel Echenberg. *Canadian Journal of African Studies* (Montreal), vol. 3, no. 3 (1969), p. 531-61. maps.

Echenberg provides a detailed account of an attempt to set up an Islamic state in Dafina, a region straddling Mali and Burkina Faso, shortly before the onset of French colonial rule.

41 **Kokona. Essai d'histoire structurale.** (Kokona. Essay on structural history.)
Kalo Antoine Millogo. Stuttgart, Germany: F. Steiner, 1990. 231p. map. bibliog.

A comprehensive study of Kotedugu's history, the customs of its Bobo and other ethnic groups, their cosmology and religious beliefs. Over half of the work deals with the place of masks in Bobo society, their significance and rôle in ritual dances.

42   **La légende royale des Kouroumba.** (The royal legend of the Kurumba.)
Wilhelm Staude.   *Journal de la Société des Africanistes* (Paris), vol. 31,
no. 2 (1961), p. 209-59.
A detailed examination of several oral versions of the origins, arrival, and installation
of the Kurumba monarchy in the Mengao and Laroum regions. Serious research on
this ethnic group commenced only in 1938, and was interrupted by the Second World
War.

43   **Liptako speaks. History from oral tradition in Africa.**
Paul Irwin.   Princeton, New Jersey: Princeton University Press, 1981.
221p. bibliog.
An intimate and fascinating record of the oral history of Liptako, a small pre-colonial
Fulani emirate centred around Dori. The author's work in reconciling contrary
accounts of expert testimony (often by the same individuals but in different settings)
spurred him to consider methodological issues on the value of oral tradition.

44   **Mission au Mossi et au Gourounsi.** (Mission to the Mossi and Gurunsi.)
Paul Voulet.   Paris: Chapelot, 1898. 320p.
A first-hand account of the ill-fated Voulet-Chanoine expedition into Mossi and
Gurunsi areas, which formed a prelude to the French military occupation. See also
Paul Voulet and Julien Chanoine, 'Dans la boucle du Niger, au Mossi et au Gourounsi'
(At the bend of the Niger, in Mossi and Gurunsi areas), *Bulletin de la Société de
Géographie de Lille* (Lille), vol. 29 (1898), p. 109-41; Julien Chanoine, 'Mission
Voulet-Chanoine' (The Voulet-Chanoine mission), *Bulletin de la Société de Géographie
Commerciale* (Paris), vol. 20 (1898), p. 220-79. For another account of an early
explorer in this region, see Henri Labouret, *Monteil, explorateur et soldat* (Monteil,
explorer and soldier) (Paris: Berger-Levrault, 1937. 304p.).

45   **The political organization of traditional gold mining: the western Loby,
c.1850 to c.1901.**
B. M. Perinbaum.   *Journal of African History* (Cambridge), vol. 29,
no. 3 (1988), p. 437-62. map. bibliog.
A study of nineteenth-century gold-mining in the Lobi regions of southern Burkina
Faso. The author emphasizes the fact that gold-mining was not associated with highly
centralized polities, but was almost exclusively in the hands of animist lineages,
including Mande, grouped in small towns, despite their suzerainty to the Kong
Wattara.

46   **Souvenirs de guerre d'un 'tirailleur sénégalais'.** (War recollections of a
Senegalese infantryman.)
Joseph Issoufou.   Paris: Harmattan, 1989. 199p.
Recollections by a former Prime Minister of his military service in France's colonial
armies, including during the Second World War.

47 **Un vent de folie? Le conflit armé dans une population sans état: les Lobi de Haute-Volta.** (A wind of madness? Armed conflict in a stateless people: the Lobi of Upper Volta.)
P. Bonnafe (et al.). In: *Guerres de lignages et guerres d'états en Afrique*, edited by J. Bazin, E. Terray. Paris: Editions des Archives Contemporaines, 1982, p. 73-141. map.

An attempt to understand the fierce Lobi resistance to French occupation through an examination of their history and culture. Such a resistance would not normally have been expected from the Lobi who do not possess centralized structures above the extended family unit. For an early work on the Lobi, see Henri Labouret, *Nouvelles notes sur les tribus du rameau Lobi: leurs migrations, leurs évolution, leurs parler et ceux de leurs voisins* (New notes on the tribes of the Lobi wedge: their migrations, their evolution, their language, and that of their neighbours) (Dakar, IFAN, 1923. 296p.). Other important research on the Lobi includes Georges Savonnet, 'La colonisation du pays Koulango par les Lobi de Haute Volta' (The colonization of the Koulango by the Lobi of Upper Volta), *Cahiers d'Outre-mer* (Bordeaux), vol. 15, no. 57 (Jan.-March 1962), p. 79-102.

# Mossi history

48 **Ainsi on a assassiné tous les Mosse.** (Thus all of the Mossi were killed.)
Frédéric Titinga Pacéré. Sherbrooke, Canada: Naaman, 1972. 172p. bibliog.

Pacéré, a prolific author and eminent lawyer outlines the manner in which Mossi life, tradition and 'spirituality' were disrupted and eventually destroyed by the imposition of French colonial rule. The study focuses on the special rôle of the Mogho Naba, and on the kingdoms of Tenkodogo, Wargaye, Bousma and Biounga, and includes an important bibliography. For another perspective, see Joseph I. Conombo, *M'ba Tinga: traditions des Mosse dans l'Empire du Mogho-Naba* (M'ba Tinga: Traditions of the Mossi in the empire of Mogho Naba) (Paris: Harmattan, 1989. 185p.). The latter, written by a former Prime Minister, outlines recollections of Mossi life and customs twenty-one years after the French conquest of the empire.

49 **Alfred Diban, premier chrétien de Haute-Volta.** (Alfred Diban, the first Christian of Upper Volta.)
Joseph Ki Zerbo. Paris: Editions du CERF, 1983. 148p.

The story of Alfred Diban, born around 1875, who converted to Christianity to become a priest. In 1975 he made a pilgrimage to Rome and was honoured by Pope Paul VI. The author is Diban's son and one of Africa's best-known historians. The study relies on the archival material of the White Fathers, and an oral transcript of Diban himself, translated from More.

50 **The changing status of the 'Emperor of the Mossi' under colonial rule and since independence.**
Elliott P. Skinner. In: *West African chiefs*, edited by Michael Crowder, Obaro Ikime. New York: Africana, 1970, p. 98-123. bibliog.

A study of the changing social and political rôles of Mossi chiefs, especially the Mogho Naba, during French colonial rule and the first two post-independence administrations in Ouagadougou. Skinner, an anthropologist, is the foremost American scholar of the Mossi. He reveals that notwithstanding the greatly diminished political and sacramental rôle of the Mogha Naba, the latter still retained widespread respect and authority among his subjects. However, whenever Mossi chiefs, including the Mogho Naba, have involved themselves in political activity, they have lost popular support. See also the author's 'The Mossi and traditional Sudanese history', *Journal of Negro History* (Washington, DC), vol. 43, no. 2 (April 1958), p. 121-31.

51 **Chroniques d'un cercle de l'A.O.F.: receuil d'archives du poste de Ouahigouya, 1908-1941.** (Chronicles of an A.O.F. circle: extracts from the Ouahigouya post, 1908-1941.)
Yves J. Marchal. Paris: ORSTOM, 1980. maps.

A collection of extracts from monthly and annual official reports of the Ouahigouya district to the Lieutenant Governor's office in Ouagadougou. These are presented chronologically for the period 1908-41, with little comment beyond footnotes aimed at explaining the significance of the text. The data reveal a great deal about the work and concerns of the French administration in the district, and about local reactions to the various demands made upon them.

52 **L'Empire du Mogho-Naba. Coutumes des Mossi de Haute-Volta.** (The Mogho-Naba Empire. Mossi customs in Upper Volta.)
A. A. Dim Delobsom. Paris: Editions Domat-Montchrestien, 1932. 303p. maps.

Delobsom's study is one of the two most influential early works (the other one being Tauxier's – see item no. 77) on the history, customs, cosmology and traditional law of the Mossi. It was written by the son of a chief from Sao, a descendant of the founder of the Ouagadougou kingdom, and many respondents in Burkina Faso still refer all researchers to this work. Since the 1960s, however, the historical accuracy of the dates in it has been challenged, since they rest on uncritical acceptance of oral tradition which conflicts with records of other groups in the vicinity of the Mossi. For oral history collected on the origins of the Ouagadougou kingdom, see Liliane Diallo, 'Aux origines du Wubri-tenga de Guilongou après une tradition orale recueillie dans ces villages' (On the origins of the Wubri-tenga of Guilongou according to an oral tradition collected in these villages), *Genève-Afrique* (Geneva), vol. 23, no. 2 (1985), p. 7-36.

53 **Une enquête historique en pays Mossi.** (A historical enquiry in Mossi country.)
Robert Pageard. *Journal des Africanistes* (Paris), vol. 35, no. 1 (1965), p. 11-66. maps. bibliog.

An historical overview of eight lesser-studied Mossi districts, which includes an attempt to reconcile chronological dates and king/chief lists.

54 **La formation de Ouahigouya.** (The formation of Ouahigouya.)
Michel Izard. *Journal de la Société des Africanistes* (Paris), vol. 41,
no. 2 (1971), p. 151-87. bibliog.

An account of the foundation of Ouahigouya circa 1780, by Naaba (Chief) Kango, the
26th sovereign of the Yatenga, and of the town's evolution since. The study focuses on
the early years, the lineages that established themselves in the town, and the rôle
played by their progeny in the institutionalization of a central administration.

55 **Gens de pouvoir, gens de terre: les institutions politiques de l'ancien
royaume du Yatenga.** (People of power, people of the earth: the political
institutions of the ancient kingdom of Yatenga.)
Michel Izard. Cambridge, England; Paris: Cambridge University Press,
1985. 594p. maps. bibliog.

A massive study of the political, social and economic structures, and of the practices of
the second most important Mossi kingdom of Yatenga over three centuries of
independence. Established in the mid-sixteenth century in the north-central region of
Burkina Faso, shortly before falling under French rule in 1895, Yatenga occupied a
territory of 12,300 square kilometres and had a population of half a million people. In
the late eighteenth century a system of central government evolved, resting on a
balance of power between Mossi chiefs, who were heads of the dominant populations
in the kingdom, and earth-priests, descendants of the indigenous populations who
retained rights over their lands, with the Yatenga Naba at the apex of power. Despite
dynastic crises, intermittent droughts and wars, stability and trade were maintained.
Izard is France's foremost scholar on Burkina Faso, and is the author of numerous
other works. This book is regarded as the definitive study of Yatenga; a briefer version
may be found in his *Le Yatenga précolonial: un ancien royaume du Burkina*
(Precolonial Yatenga: a former kingdom of Burkina) (Paris: Karthala, 1985. 164p.
maps. bibliog.). See also Izard's 'Le royaume Mossi de Yatenga' (Yatenga's Mossi
kingdom), in *Princes et serviteurs du royaume: cinq études de monarchies africaines*
(Princes and servants of the kingdom: five studies of African monarchies) edited by
Claude Tardits (Paris: Société d'Ethnologie, 1987, p. 59-106). For the evolution of 426
Yatenga villages and 2,194 urban quarters, and the factors that brought about the earth-
priesthood, metallurgy, long-distance trade, and a centralized court, see his 'Quatre
siècles d'histoire d'une région du Moogo' (Four centuries of the history of a Mossi
region), *Journal des Africanistes* (Paris), vol. 58, no. 2 (1988), p. 7-51 (with English
summary). *Traditions historiques des villages du Yatenga* (Historical traditions of
Yatenga villages) (Paris: CNRS, 1965, 223p.) surveys the oral traditions concerning
the origins of 113 villages in the district of Gourcey. For Yatenga's foreign policy, see
'La politique extérieure d'un royaume africain: le Yatenga au XIXe siècle' (The
foreign policy of an African kingdom: Yatenga in the 19th century), *Cahiers d'Etudes
Africaines* (Paris), vol. 22, no. 3/4 (1982), p. 363-85.

56 **Histoire et coutumes royales des Mossi de Ouagadougou.** (History and
royal customs of the Mossi of Ouagadougou.)
Yamba Tiendrebeogo, edited by Robert Pageard. Ouagadougou:
Presses Africaines, 1964. 206p. maps.

This book, by the Naba Adgha (an official at the Mogho Naba court in Ougadougou in
charge of oral tradition), is composed of two parts: a reprint of his article (also edited
by Pageard) 'Histoire traditionnelle des Mossi de Ouagadougou' (Traditional history of
the Mossi of Ouagadougou), *Journal de la Société des Africanistes* (Paris), vol. 33, no.

1 (1963), p. 7-46; followed by his account of the organizational structure of the ancient kingdom and the rôle of tradition and authority within it. See also Robert Pageard, 'Une enquête historique en pays Mossi' (An historical inquiry in Mossi country), *Journal de la Société des Africanistes* (Paris), vol. 35, no. 1 (1965), p. 11-66.

57 **Islam et colonisation au Yatenga (1897-1950).** (Islam and the colonization of Yatenga, 1897-1950.)
Hamidou Diallo. *Le Mois en Afrique* (Paris). vol 21, no. 237/8 (Nov. 1985), p. 33-42.
An attempt to explain the massive inroads made by Islam in Yatenga since the advent of colonial rule; until then it had been fiercely resisted by the Mossi who were deeply attached to their animist beliefs. According to the author, the opening up of the country to modern commerce and trade presented practical advantages for those who converted to the faith of the dominant Muslim commercial groups.

58 **Late nineteenth-century military technology in Upper Volta.**
Myron Joel Echenberg. *Journal of African History* (London), vol. 12, no. 2 (1971), p. 141-54.
A study of the rôle of military innovations in the establishment and expansion of the Mossi states through an investigation of military organization and warfare technology in four such polities. Among these Echenberg notes that it was the use of cavalry by the Mossi that played the decisive rôle in their conquests of territory, giving them an aura of invincibility. By the late nineteenth century, however, the prevalence of firearms in the region disturbed the established order.

59 **Mogho Naba Wobgho: la résistance du royaume mossi de Ouagadougou.** (Mogho Naba Wobgho: the resistance of the Mossi kingdom of Ouagadougou.)
Françoise Bretout. Paris: ABC, 1976. 92p. map. bibliog.
A biography of Mogho Naba Wobgho and his efforts to ward off French designs on his dominions, including the Voulet-Chanoine mission.

60 **The Mossi and the Akan states.**
Ivor Wilks. In: *History of West Africa*, edited by J. F. A. Ajayi, Michael Crowder. Harlow, England: Longman, 1985. 3rd edn., p. 465-502. map. bibliog.
A history written by an eminent historian, of the region between the two Volta rivers between the years 1400 and 1800.

61 **The Mossi Kingdoms.**
Dominique Zahan. In: *West African Kingdoms in the nineteenth century*, edited by Daryll Forde, P. M. Kaberry. London: Oxford University Press, 1967, p. 152-78. map. bibliog.
In this early study of Mossi history, social structures, organization and social practices, the author notes the continued reticence of many of those interviewed to provide information, and the slow erosion of tradition that prevents a reconstruction of the Mossi past. The article stresses Yatenga in particular, and includes a detailed outline of

the Mossi economy, administration, military and judicial administration, and the sources of royal power.

62 **The Mossi of Burkina Faso: the political development of a Sudanic people.**
Elliott Percival Skinner.   Prospect Heights, Illinois: Waveland Press, 1989. 236p. map.

This reprint of the classic 1964 work published by Stanford University Press is a study of the political organization, social structures, economy, legal and administrative system, religion and warfare practices of the Mossi as they evolved over the centuries and up to the eve of independence. Virtually all other historic kingdoms of the Western Sudan atrophied or disappeared with the advent of colonialism, the Mossi being the only people to maintain their traditional structures and reverence for the Mogho Naba. Skinner traces the variables that served to sustain the Mossi system of values for so long, noting that it was only the profound post-Second World War reforms that began to erode traditional authority.

63 **Organisation politique traditionnelle et évolution politique des Mossi de Ouagadougou.** (Traditional political organization and political evolution of the Mossi of Ouagadougou.)
Gomkoudougou Victor Kabore.   Paris: CNRS, 1966. 224p. bibliog.

Kabore offers a comprehensive description of the ancient kingdom of Ouagadougou. The kingdom was kept stable and intact through a hierarchical system of social and political power at the centre of which stood the Mogho Naba, his centralized Court and state administration. The loyalty of the conquered indigenous populations was retained by integrating into the array of power of their chiefs with religious authority.

64 **Prémisses d'un état moderne? Les projets coloniaux dans le bassin des Volta, 1897-1960.** (Premises for a modern state? Colonial projects in the Volta basins.)
Jean-Yves Marchal.   *Cahiers d'Etudes Africaines* (Paris), vol. 26, no. 3 (1986), p. 403-20. bibliog.

The roots of mass Mossi migration to neighbouring states are traced to French labour policy during the colonial era in Ouagadougou. Post-independent régimes have not been able to halt the drain on the population. An English summary is included.

65 **Reflections on the early history of the Mossi–Dagomba group of states.**
John Donelly Fage.   In: *The historian in tropical Africa*, edited by Jan Vansina, Raymond Mauny, L. V. Thomas.   London: Oxford University Press, 1964, p. 177-91.

An early revisionist approach by a top Africanist, suggesting that the discipline's Mossi-centred fixation on the history of Mossi–Dagomba states astride the Ghana–Burkina Faso border had resulted in serious misinterpretations of their early history. Specifically, the foundation dates of the Mossi states suggested by previous scholars (eleventh century according to Delafosse and Delobsom; thirteenth century according to Tauxier) are 'very much too early' with the end of the fifteenth century a more likely date. A reinterpretation of the early history of the region should give 'full weight to the source material available for the southern states' (p. 176). Fage's contentions have since been accepted by most historians.

66 **Le royaume du Yatenga et ses forgerons: une recherche d'histoire du peuplement.** (The Yatenga kingdom and its metal-workers: historical research of a people.)
Michel Izard. In: *Métallurgies africaines: nouvelles contributions*, edited by N. Echard. Paris: Société des Africanistes, 1983, p. 256-79.
In many African societies, metal-workers were regarded as a special caste with magic powers, valued for their craft, feared for their special powers, and at times despised as well. Izard analyses the evolution and rôle played by metal-workers in the Yatenga kingdom.

67 **Textes historiques oraux des Mosi méridionaux.** (Oral history texts of the central Mosi.)
Junzo Kawado. Tokyo: Institut de Recherches sur les Langues et Cultures d'Asie et de l'Afrique, 1985. 307p. bibliog.
A verbatim translation from More to French of ancestral recitals of the chiefs of the Tenkodogo, Lalge and Ouagadougou (in the first instance in two versions), accompanied by editorial comment. In a subsequent article the author analyses the dynastic genealogy of the royal line of Tenkodogo, and the myths and reality associated with it. See 'Histoire orale et imaginaire du passé' (Oral and imaginary history of the past), *Revue de l'Institut de Sociologie* (Brussels), no. 3/4 (1988), p. 127-36. bibliog. See also the other collected oral traditions presented in L. Diallo, 'Collecte, parmi les autochtones, de traditions orales concernant l'époque de Naaba Wubri' (Collection, among the natives, of oral traditions of the Naaba Wubri area), *Journal of Asian and African Studies* (Tokyo). no. 35 (1988), p. 113-56.

68 **Towards a history of the Yatenga Mossi.**
Dominique Zahan. In: *French perspectives in African studies*, edited by Pierre Alexandre. Oxford: Oxford University Press, 1973, p. 96-117.
A reconstruction of the origins of the Yatenga kingdom in which Zahan notes that there is little evidence beyond oral history for the period prior to 1894, and that many of these recitations are often uncritically accepted, resulting in the falsification of Yatenga history. Indeed, 'whenever one tries to get information on the traditions of chiefship among the Mossi many respondents simply send the ethnographer back to the works of Tauxier and Dim Delobsom . . . [who] viewed the evolution and functioning of these societies through a prism of occidental logic' (p. 116).

69 **Les Yarsés du royaume de Ouagadougou: l'écrit et l'orale.** (The Yarse of the Ougadougou kingdom: written and oral sources.)
Anne-Marie Duperray. *Cahiers d'Etudes Africaines* (Paris), vol. 25, no. 2 (1985), p. 179-212. bibliog.
A study of the Yarse strata, who are distinguished by their religion (Islam), former occupation (caravaneering) and privileged standing in society. The author examines contradictory oral traditions, one of which maintains that the Yarse came from Mande

19

**History.** Mossi history

areas, changed their language to More, and intermarried with noble Mossi lineages. The article is summarized in English.

**Haut-Sénégal–Niger.** (Upper Senegal–Niger.)
*See* item no. 5.

# The Peoples

## General

70 **Ethnic identification in the Voltaic region: problems of the perception of 'tribe' and 'tribal society'.**
Jan Ovesen. Uppsala, Sweden: University of Uppsala, 1985. 31p. (Working Papers in African Studies no. 13).
An overview of the problems of defining ethnic groups, especially the Bobo and Lobi. This is because ethnographers 'have rendered the native names differently and have classified the various groups of people into different categories according to different variables', and because 'the people themselves appear to give as confusing a picture of the ethnic situation in the area' (p. 1).

71 **La population de la Haute-Volta au recensement de décembre 1975.** (The population of Upper Volta at the December 1975 general census.)
M. F. Courel (et al.). *Cahiers d'Outre-mer* (Bordeaux), vol. 32, no. 125 (Jan.-March 1979), p. 39-65. maps.
A demographic study (with English summary) based on the first census of the country. All aspects of the population are reported on, including migrant labour patterns. For the results of the follow-up 1985 census, grouped by province, department and other categories, see *Recensement général de la population, 1985: structure par âge et sexe des villages du Burkina Faso* (Ouagadougou: Institut National de la Statistique et de la Démographie, 1988. 330p.; *Analyse des résultats définitifs: deuxième recensement général de la population* (Ouagadougou: Institut National de la Statistique et de la Démographie, 1990. 318p.).

# The Mossi

## 72 Economic change and Mossi acculturation.
Peter B. Hammond.  In: *Continuity and change in African cultures*,
edited by William R. Bascom, Melville J. Herskovitz.    Chicago,
Illinois: University of Chicago Press, 1959, p. 238-56.

Hammond provides a compact summary of Mossi culture, economic organization,
social and political structures and religious beliefs. This is a prelude to an analysis of
the acculturation experiences of 5,000 Mossi farmers resettled in newly developed land
in neighbouring French Soudan (now Mali) without the institutions on which they had
depended for security, with a water supply not dependent on the supposed
supernatural powers of earth custodians but from a dam, and in isolation from kinsmen
and ancestral spirits.

## 73 Une famille Mossi. (A Mossi family.)
Suzanne Lallemand.    Paris: CNRS, 1977. 380p. bibliog.

Filling a gap in scholarship on the much-studied Mossi, Lallemand focuses her work on
the Mossi family. Based on extensive fieldwork, the book outlines the nature of
courtship, pre- and post-nuptial conjugal relations, the marriage ceremony, the duties
of each partner, family consumption of goods, education and raising of children,
relations with co-wives and the extended family. For an account of related issues in
English, see Elliott Percival Skinner's 'The effect of co-residence of sister's sons on
African corporate patrilineal descent groups', *Cahiers d'Etudes Africaines* (Paris), vol.
4 (1964), p. 464-78; and 'Intergenerational conflict among the Mossi: father and son',
*Journal of Conflict Resolution* (Lawrence, Kansas), (March 1961), p. 55-60. See also
Kathryn C. Mason, 'Co-wife relationships can be amicable as well as conflictual: the
case study of the Moose of Burkina Faso', *Canadian Journal of African Studies*
(Toronto), vol. 22, no. 3 (1988), p. 615-24. For female body-markings among the
Mossi see Suzanne Lallemand, 'Entre excision et accouchement: les scarifications des
filles Mossi du Burkina' (Between excision and childbirth: the scarification of Mossi
girls in Burkina), *Archiv für Völkerkunde* (Vienna), no. 40 (1986), p. 63-74.

## 74 The Mossi. Essay on the manners and customs of the Mossi people in the Western Sudan.
Eugene P. Mangin, translated from the German by Arlane Brunel,
Elliott Percival Skinner.    New Haven, Connecticut: Human Relations
Area Files, 1959. 141p.

This pioneering and still valuable study of Mossi society, culture, traditions and
religion was originally published in *Anthropos* (Vienna), vol. 9 (1914), p. 98-124, 477-
93, 705-36; vol. 10/11 (1915-16), p. 187-217.

## 75 Mossi joking.
Peter B. Hammond.    *Ethnology* (Pittsburgh), vol. 3, no. 3 (July 1964),
p. 259-67. bibliog.

Systematizing anthropological thinking about humour, Hammond suggests that jokes
have five structural attributes and also serve as 'an adjustive mechanism . . . of
communications control, and the culturally harmless catharsis of potentially disruptive

emotions' (p. 266). See also Peter Collett, 'Mossi salutations', *Semiotica* (Amsterdam), vol. 45, no. 3/4 (1983), p. 191-248.

76  **The Mossi** *pogsioure.*
    Elliott Percival Skinner.   *Man* (London), no. 60 (Feb. 1960), p. 20-73.

The importance of giving gifts to cement social relationships in traditional societies is explored through a study of the Mossi institution of *pogsioure* whereby chiefs give away women as wives to members of their lineages, other worthy clients, and even strangers who are thus brought into their social group.

77  **Le Noir du Yatenga: pays Mossi et Gourounsi.** (The Black of Yatenga: Mossi and Gurunsi country.)
    Louis Tauxier.   Paris: Larose, 1912. 796p.

Written by a colonial administrator who served in Burkina Faso (1913-16) this was the pioneering, and for half a century the key study of Yatenga. The work is a comprehensive study of Mossi, Gurunsi and Fulani history, culture, customs, religion, agricultural practices and trade. The book includes king-lists, and appendices of Bambara and Mossi (two dialects) vocabulary. Tauxier has more recently been taken to task for uncritically accepting at face value oral history and the chronology of Yatenga history. See also Tauxier's *Nouvelles notes sur le Mossi et le Gourounsi* (New notes on the Mossi and the Gurunsi) (Paris: Larose, 1924. 206p.).

78  **Rational self-interest or solidarity: the predominance of non-economic motives among the Moose of Burkina Faso.**
    Alan Page Fisk.   In: *Structures of life: the four elementary forms of human relations*, edited by Alan Page Fisk.   New York: Free Press, 1991, p. 231-307. bibliog.

A far-ranging synthesis of social theory arguing that whenever people relate to each other they organize their social relations 'on the basis of four elementary psychological models'. The author uses the Mossi case-study to illustrate that their lack of economic drive is a function of their cultural ethos. See also Fisk's 'Relativity within Moose [Mossi] culture: four incommensurable models for social relationships', *Ethos* (Berkeley), vol. 18, no. 2 (1990), p. 180-204.

79  **Le retour de l'ancêtre.** (The return of the ancestor.)
    Doris Bonnet.   *Journal des Africanistes* (Paris), vol. 51, no. 1/2 (1981), p. 133-47.

An analysis (with English summary) of Mossi beliefs that ancestors can return via descendants on the agnatic line. Children's sicknesses are sometimes explained by diviners as either due to the inability to identify the returning ancestor or due to two spirits trying to return via the body of one child. For more detail on Mossi concepts of child illnesses, infertility, and traditional medical treatments of maladies see Doris Bonnet, *Corps biologique, corps social: procréation et maladies de l'enfant en pays mossi, Burkina Faso* (Biological body, social body: procreation and illness of children in Mossi country, Burkina Faso) (Paris: ORSTOM, 1988. 138p.).

80 **Les secrets des sorciers noirs.** (The secrets of Black sorcerers.)
   A. A. Dim Delobsom. Paris: Emile Nourry, 1934, 298p.

One of the first works on Mossi secret societies, magic, fetishism and treatment of
diseases, by a Mossi *evolué* and descendant of the dynasty which founded the
Ouagadougou kingdom.

81 **Trade and markets among the Mossi people.**
   Elliott Percival Skinner.   In: *Markets in Africa*, edited by Paul
   Bohannan and George Dalton.   Evanston, Illinois: Northwestern
   University Press, 1962, p. 237-78.

A description of Mossi trade and commerce both in pre-colonial days and after the
onset of French rule. The author draws on nineteenth-century accounts (especially by
German explorer Barth) about caravan routes through Mossi territory and the conduct
of trade in Mossi trading centres. In the contemporary era Skinner refers to the 'highly
unorganized' trade with Ghana and Côte d'Ivoire, with the goods changing hands
being 'the same as those traded in pre-European times'. There then follows a detailed
account of a typical Mossi market, with all its social, ritual and economic aspects.

82 **Traditional power of Mossi *nanamse* of Upper Volta.**
   Jean Bigtarma Zoanga.   In: *The nomadic alternative*, edited by
   W. Weissleder.   The Hague: Mouton, 1978, p. 215-46. bibliog.

Zoanga analyses of the importance of kinship in political authority, and the continuing
relevance of traditional chiefs (known as *nanamse*, plural of *naba*). The author traces
the powers of chiefs to the pre-colonial era, and to illustrate the continued rôle of
chiefly authority he includes a translation of a poetic song broadcast over Burkina's
radio station, with extensive commentary on the cultural values implicit in it. For the
role of royal drums as transmitters of chiefly orders, see Junzo Kawado, 'La
panégyrique royale tambourine mossi: un instrument de control idéologique' (The
Mossi royal drums panegyric: instruments of ideological control), *Revue Française
d'Histoire d'Outre Mer* (Paris), vol. 68, no. 250/53 (1981), p. 131-53.

83 **Women's virtue and the structure of the Mossi *zaka*.**
   Marta Rohatynskyj.   *Canadian Journal of African Affairs* (Toronto),
   vol. 22, no. 3 (1988), p. 528-51.

Labour and life-cycle, gender issues, witchcraft and family relations in a Mossi *zaka*,
the basic productive unit of agnates, their wives and children. For Mossi traditional
marriages, compared to those of other neighbouring groups, see Robert Pageard,
'Contribution a l'étude de l'exogamie dans la société mossi traditionnelle' (Contribu-
tion to the study of exogamy in traditional Mossi society), *Journal de la Société des
Africanistes* (Paris), vol. 36, no. 1 (1966), p. 109-40. For social power and control in
Mossi domestic life, a function of status, gender and age, see Marc-Eric Gruenais,
'Aînés, aînées, cadets, cadettes: les relations aînés/cadets chez les Mossi du centre
Burkina Faso' (Eldest, youngest: the eldest/youngest relationship among the Mossi of
central Burkina Faso), in: *Age, pouvoir et société en Afrique Noire*, edited by Marc
Abeles, Chantal Collard (Paris: Karthala, 1985. 330p.).

84 **Yatenga: technology in the culture of a West African kingdom.**
Peter B. Hammond. New York: Macmillan, 1966. 331p.
Based on anthropological fieldwork, this is a study of the intimate connection between
technology and Mossi culture in their economic organization, social, political and
religious beliefs. The work, illustrated by thirty-three plates, integrates several
theoretical positions hitherto regarded as antithetical, and suggests a more dynamic
way of analysing non-Western peoples. As Hammond notes, 'the primacy attached to
redistribution and reciprocity as mechanisms for the allocation of both productive and
consumptive goods . . . is causally related to technological factors . . . the economic
system of the Mossi is organized as it is . . . because it works better than any
alternative system to meet the Mossi's cultural needs and thus foster their survival'
(p. 206-7).

# The Lobi

85 **Anthropologie du sang en Afrique: essai d'hématologie symbolique chez
les Lobi du Burkina Faso et de Côte d'Ivoire.** (The anthropology of blood
in Africa: essay on the symbolism of haematology among the Lobi of
Burkina Faso and Côte d'Ivoire.)
Michelle Cros. Paris: Harmattan, 1990. 298p. map. bibliog.
Cros provides an erudite study of all aspects of the rôle of blood among the Lobi. The
study examines the Lobi cosmology of liquid components of men and women
(including menstrual blood and breast milk) and explores the phenomena of birth,
sickness and death, all perceived as being connected with blood, and the forced
haemorrhages practised by Lobi sorcerers to expiate 'bad blood'. The work, which is
profusely illustrated with plates and drawings, includes a section on ritual sacrifices,
and an extensive bibliography.

86 **Le chasseur Lobi: une étude ethno-sociologique.** (The Lobi hunter: an
ethno-sociological study.)
Helga Diallo. Vienna: Acta Ethnologica et Linguistica, 1978. 78p.
A study of the Lobi hunter and his prey, and a specific life-history of one hunter.

87 **Death, property and the ancestors. A study of mortuary customs of the
LoDagaa of West Africa.**
Jack Goody. Stanford, California: Stanford University Press, 1962.
452p. bibliog.
A comprehensive study of death and funeral rites, inheritance and succession customs
among the Lobi along the Ghana–Burkina Faso border, including a minutely detailed
account of each mortuary rite.

88 **Un exemple d'indépendence et de résistance religieuse: les hommes et les dieux Lobi.** (An example of independence and religious resistance: the Lobi and their gods.)
Michelle Cros. *Mondes et Développement* (Paris), vol. 17, no. 65 (1989), p. 59-65. map.

The Lobi have resisted to this day the penetration of imported religions, with neither Islam nor Christianity gaining many converts among them, despite considerable missionary activity and contact with Muslim traders. When some do convert, it is usually in urban areas, aimed at garnering specific tangible material gains. The fact that the Lobi strenuously resisted the colonial intrusion has allowed them to preserve their religious identity to this day. An English summary is included.

89 **The orchestration of Lobi funeral rituals.**
Jan Ovesen. *Folk* (Copenhagen), vol. 28 (1986), p. 87-107. map. bibliog.

A detailed analysis of Lobi perceptions and representations of death, and their elaborate funeral rituals. See also Pierre Bonnafe, Michele Fieloux 'Le dédain de la mort et la force du cadavre: sorcellure et purification d'un meurtrier Lobi' (The disdain for death and the strength of a corpse: sorcery and the purification of a Lobi murderer), *Etudes Rurales* (Paris), no. 95-6 (1984), p. 43-62.

90 **Organisation sociale des Lobi: une société bilinéaire du Burkina Faso et Côte d'Ivoire.** (Social organisation among the Lobi: a bilinear society in Burkina Faso and Côte d'Ivoire.)
Cécile de Rouville. Paris: Harmattan, 1987. p. 259. maps. bibliog.

A concise but comprehensive study of Lobi social structures, clan and class systems, marriage and household organization, with extensive kinship tables. Originating in northwest Ghana, the Lobi migrated into contemporary Burkina Faso at the end of the eighteenth century, settling along the sparsely populated border with Côte d'Ivoire. They live as extended families, with no larger political structures: social order is assured by the head of the extended family, and by a series of cult interdictions. Despite foreign influences the Lobi have retained their cultural identity. Their resistance to colonial rule, Christianity, Islam, and modernity, and their strong individualism, has given their society a strength unique in Africa. See also Madeleine Père, *Les Lobis: tradition et changement; Burkina Faso* (The Lobi: tradition and change in Burkina Faso) (Laval, France: Siloe, 1988. 2 vols), which analyses the forces of tradition and change in Lobi society. For a reprint of the 1956 classic by anthropologist Jack Goody, see *The social organization of the Lo Willi* (London: Oxford University Press, 1967. 123p.).

91 **Pour une approche écologique des guerres lobi.** (For an ecological approach to the Lobi wars.)
Michelle Cros, Daniel Dory. *Cultures et Développement* (Louvain), vol. 16, no. 3-4 (1984), p. 465-84. bibliog.

An analysis of the reasons for the arrival of the Lobi in their current habitat under ecological and slave-raiding pressures.

92  **Les tribus du rameau Lobi.** (The tribes of the Lobi branch.)
Henri Labouret.  Paris: Institut d'Ethnologie, 1931. 510p. maps.
bibliog.

This is the classic monograph on the Lobi. Interspersed with thirty-one plates, it is an
encyclopaedic survey of the habitat, history, economy, art and ethnology of the Lobi,
and a detailed study of their clans, religious practices, funerary rites and the rôle of
magic amongst them.

# The Fulani

93  **Le chemin des Peuls du Boobola.** (The road of the Boobola Fulani.)
Michel Benoit.   Paris: ORSTOM, 1979. 207p. maps. bibliog.

A survey of a Fulani pastoral community in western Burkina Faso near the Mali
border, the foundations of their seasonal migrations and transhumance patterns, their
economy and art. See also the author's *Nature peul du Yatenga* (Fulani life in Yatenga)
– see item no. 96. For a study of transhumance patterns, pasturage and the subsistence
economy in the northwest, see Michel Benoit. *Introduction à la géographie des aires
pastorales soudaniennes de Haute Volta* (Introduction to the geography of the Sudanese
pastoral areas of Upper Volta) (Paris: ORSTOM, 1977. 93p.). For the Tuareg, see
Erik Guignard, *Faits et modèles de parenté chez les Touareg Udalen de Haute-Volta*
(Facts and kinship models of the Tuareg Udalen of Upper Volta) (Paris: Harmattan,
1988. 259p.).

94  **First find your child a good mother: the construction of self in two
African communities.**
Paul Riesman.   New Brunswick, New Jersey: Rutgers University Press,
1992. 321p. map. bibliog.

A study of parenting, child socialization and psychology, and the world outlook in two
Fulani societies. Riesman's book (completed by colleagues after his death in 1984) is
based on observations of identical child-rearing practices by the Fulani and their
former slaves with completely different outcomes, and suggests a culturally variable
relationship between identity and personality, pinpointing personality factors that may
be universal and others which are culturally defined.

95  **Love Fulani style.**
Paul Riesman.   *Society* (New Brunswick, New Jersey), vol. 10, no. 2
(Jan.-Feb. 1973), p. 27-35.

A popular account of Fulani attitudes towards love, sex and fidelity. Another article on
the Fulani outlook on life by the same author (who lived among them), is 'The art of
life in a West African community: formality and spontaneity in Fulani inter-personal
relationships', *Journal of African Studies* (Los Angeles), vol. 2 (Spring 1975), p. 39-63.

96 **Nature peul du Yatenga: remarques sur le pastoralisme en pays mossi.**
(Fulani life in Yatenga: remarks on pastoralism in Mossi country.)
Michel Benoit.    Paris: ORSTOM, 1982. 176p. maps. bibliog.

A study of the pastoral way of life in a region where a progressive growth in both cattle
and human densities has exhausted available resources leading to soil, pasturage and
water resource degradation, and an extension of the nomadization belt further south to
meet the needs of the pastoral peoples. For a similar work see Henri Barral, *Les
populations nomades de Oudalan et leur espace pastoral* (The nomadic people of the
Oudalan and their pastoral space) (Paris: ORSTOM, 1977. 120p.). The latter is a
detailed examination of the Oudalan region in the extreme north of Burkina Faso,
inhabited mostly by Fulani and Tuareg clans, and is ideally complemented by Michel
Benoit, *Le Séno-Mango ne doit pas mourir: pastoralisme, vie sauvage et protection au
Sahel* (The Seno-Mango must not die: pastoralism, wild life and protection in the
Sahel) (Paris: ORSTOM, 1984. 143p.).

97 **Nomads of the drought: Fulbe and Wodabee nomads between power and
marginalization in the Sahel of Burkina Faso and Niger Republic.**
Mette Bovin.    In: *Adaptive strategies in African arid lands*, edited by
Mette Bovin, L. Manger.    Uppsala, Sweden: Scandinavian Institute of
African Studies, 1990, p. 29-58. maps.

A survey of two Fulani subgroups studied over a period of twenty years, and the
strategies which they have adopted to survive the periodic bouts of drought in the
Sahel. These include both greater nomadization and increased sedentarization.

98 **Société et liberté chez les Peul djelgobé de Haute-Volta.** (Society and
freedom among the Djelgobe Fulani of Upper Volta.)
Paul Riesman.    Paris: Mouton, 1974. 261p. bibliog.

A study of a group of Fulani in northern Burkina Faso, their social structure, castes,
lineages, religion and nomadic way of life. The pioneering work on the Fulani was
written by Louis Tauxier (q.v.), better known for his work on the Mossi: *Moeurs et
histoire des Peuls* (Mores and history of the Fulani) (Paris: Payot, 1938. 422p.).

99 **Views on education and health as expressed by herdsmen of the Voltaic
Sahel.**
Jacques Bugnicourt.    *African Environment* (Dakar), no. 14-16 (1980),
p. 449-56.

Fascinating verbatim transcriptions of the attitudes expressed by Fulani herdsmen on
the issues of education and health.

# The Kurumba

100 **Dessins d'enfants kurumba de Mengao.** (Drawings of Kurumba children of Mengao.)
Annemarie Schweeger-Hefel. *Journal des Africanistes* (Paris), vol. 52, no. 1/2 (1981), p. 251-64.

An examination of drawings by children (many of whom had never before used paper or pencil), revealing the manner in which they regard themselves and their relations with others. The article includes an English summary and twenty-four unnumbered pages of actual drawings. See also a similar article by Pierrette Arnaud, 'Expression graphique et milieu culturel: à propos des dessins realisés par les jeunes Kurumba' (Graphic expression and cultural context: dealing with drawings by Kurumba youth), *Journal des Africanistes* (Paris), vol. 51, no. 1/2 (1981), p. 265-76.

101 **Les insignes royaux des Kouroumba.** (The royal insignia of the Kurumba.)
Annemarie Schweeger-Hefel. *Journal des Africanistes* (Paris), vol. 32, no. 2 (1962), p. 275-323. bibliog.

An exploration of the royal legends accounting for the establishment of the Kurumba in their current habitat, followed by an analysis of their royal standards and utensils. The article is illustrated by multiple sketches and photographs by the prime scholar of the Kurumba.

102 **Die Kurumba von Lurum.** (The Kurumba of Lurum.)
Annemarie Schweeger-Hefel, Wilhelm Staude. Vienna: Verlag A. Schendl, 1972. 532p.

This comprehensive study of the Kurumba, their origins, history, social and economic structures, cosmology, religious beliefs and rituals, is supplemented by sixty-six pages of photographs. For other seminal articles by the prolific Annemarie Schweeger-Hefel, see 'Die Kunst der Kurumba' (The art of the Kurumba), *Archiv für Völkerkunde* (Vienna), vol. 17-18 (1962-3), p. 194-260, and 'Nioniosi-Kunst', *Baessler-Archiv* (Berlin), vol. 14, no. 2 (June 1966), p. 187-267.

# The Bobo/Bwa

103 **Les activités religieuses des jeunes enfants chez les Bobo.** (Religious activity of young Bobo children.)
Guy Le Moal. *Journal des Africanistes* (Paris), vol. 51, no. 1/2 (1981), p. 235-50.

An analysis (with an English summary) of Bobo attitudes towards children, including their concept that all the virtues of old age can exist in very young children. The latter are encouraged to organize into age groups between the ages of five and seven, to choose leaders and undertake religious practices including possession dances and the use of masks. Adults not only encourage such behaviour but observe it for their own pleasure.

104    **Les Bobo. Nature et fonctions des masques.** (The Bobo. The nature and functions of Masks.)
       Guy Le Moal.    Paris: ORSTOM, 1980. 535p. maps. bibliog.

The definitive study on the function and utilization of masks among the Bobo by the prime scholar of an ethnic group who inhabit an area stretching from Bobo-Dioulasso north through Mali. The author provides a survey of Bobo society and social organization, explores their religious cosmology in depth, and presents an index of animals and plants found in their habitat which play a rôle in their religious rites. The remainder of the text consists of a detailed analysis of the various kinds of masks, their accessories and symbolism, and initiation and other rites in which masks play a rôle. The work includes a large number of black-and-white plates. For the pioneering work on the Bobo see Jean Cremer, *Les Bobo: matériaux d'ethnographie et de linguistique soudanaises* (The Bobo: Sudanese ethnographic and linguistic material), edited by Henri Labouret (Paris: Geuthner, 1923-27. 4 vols).

105    **Communautés villageoises Bwa.** (Bwa village communities.)
       Jean Capron.    Paris: Institut d'Ethnologie, 1973. 379p. maps.

An ethnological study of three Bwa villages, a community straddling the Mali–Burkina Faso border, which until thirty years ago were not viewed as significantly different from the Bobo in the area. The author examines their demography, habitat, agrarian cycle, social composition and hierarchy, and cultural values.

106    **Corporate authority, exchange and personal opposition in Bobo marriages.**
       Mahir Saul.    *American Ethnologist* (Washington, DC), vol. 16, no. 1 (1989), p. 57-74. bibliog.

Saul explores the roots of corporate authority and personal autonomy concerning marriage decisions amongst the Bobo who have a double-descent system. Elders, men and women, allocate young women as wives, constraining their choice of partners in an attempt to control dependants. Opposition to this has been growing, especially with modernization, slowly increasing wealth, missionary activity and education.

107    **Une esthétique du fétiche.** (An aesthetic of fetish.)
       Michèle Coquet.    *Systèmes de Pensée en Afrique Noire* (Paris), vol. 8 (1985), p. 111-39. bibliog.

Bwa clans use a variety of objects to sum up the group's history. Through sacrificial rituals, such objects then become material evidence of succeeding historical events. See also M. J. Capron, 'Univers religieux et cohésion interne dans les communautés villageoises Bwa traditionnelles' (The religious world and internal cohesion in traditional Bwa communities) in: *African systems of thought*, edited by M. Fortes, G. Dieterlen (London: Oxford University Press, 1965. p. 291-313).

**108  Le peuplement humain de la boucle du Niger.** (Human population at the
bend of the Niger.)
Alain Froment.  Paris: ORSTOM, 1988. 194p. bibliog.

This anthropological study of the culture and customs of the populations living at the
bend of the Niger river is followed by subregional analyses, an account of the diseases
prevalent in each area, and the potential for economic development. The groups living
in these Mali–Burkina Faso border regions include the Bwa, Gurma, Fulani, Mossi and
Dogon. An extensive bibliography complements the work.

**109  Le sacrifice comme langage.** (Sacrifice as language.)
Guy Le Moal.  In: *Sous le masque de l'animal: essai sur le sacrifice en
Afrique Noire*, edited by Michel Cartry.  Paris: Presses Universitaires
de France, 1987, p. 41-87.

An interpretation of the rôle of animal sacrifices among the Bobo, and why certain
animals, of specific sex or colour, are preferred as the correct ones for the purpose of
the sacrifice. See also Guy Le Moal's 'Code sacrificiel et catégories de pensée chez les
Bobo de Haute-Volta' (Sacrificial code and thought categories among the Bobo of
Upper Volta), *Systèmes de Pensée en Afrique Noire* (Paris), vol. 6 (1983), p. 9-64; and
'Introduction à une étude du sacrifice chez les Bobo de Haute-Volta' (An introduction
to the study of sacrifices among the Bobo of Upper Volta), *Systèmes de Pensée en
Afrique Noire* (Paris), vol. 5 (1981), p. 99-125.

**110  Les voies de la rupture: veuves et orphelins, face aux tâches du deuil le
rituel funéraire bobo.** (Making a break: widows and orphans doing grief
work in Bobo funerary ceremonies.)
Guy Le Moal.  *Systèmes de Pensée en Afrique Noire* (Paris). vol. 9,
no. 1 (1986), p. 11-31; vol. 10, no. 2 (1987), p. 3-14.

An analysis (with an English summary) of the rites performed by recently widowed and
orphaned Bobo, and how feelings of loss and bereavement are handled. Rites at the
time of funerals deny the death of the soul. For rites and ritual conducted at childbirth
see Guy Le Moal, 'Naissance et rites d'identification' (Birth and identification rites),
*Archiv für Völkerkunde* (Vienna), vol. 40 (1986), p. 75-92.

# The Guin

**111  Le deuil du père, pays Guin.** (Mourning the father among the Guin.)
Michele Dacher.  *Systèmes de Pensée en Afrique Noire* (Paris), vol. 9
(1986), p. 75-103.

Dacher describes mourning rites among the Guin of southwest Burkina Faso. These do
not involve the matrilineal descent group, but only relatives through marriage and the
offspring of marriage. An English summary is included.

112 **Société lignagère et état: les Goin du Burkina Faso.** (Lineage societies and state: the Guin of Burkina Faso.)
Michele Dacher. *Genève-Afrique* (Geneva), vol. 25, no. 1 (1987), p. 43-58. map. bibliog.

Dacher argues that the family-centred orientation of the Guin has been the cause of the failure of all attempts to mobilize them collectively by successive pre- and post-independence governments. This withdrawal inwards is in part a result of the localization of power at the head of the family, accentuated by the creation during the colonial era of village chiefs who were not seen as legitimate. See also Michele Dacher, 'Identité de groupe et identité multiple: le cas des Goin du Burkina Faso', *Revue de Psychothérapie Psychoanalytique de Groupe* (Paris), no. 9-10 (1987), p. 101-15; Michele Dacher, Suzanne Lallemand, *Prix des épouses, valeurs des femmes goin du Burkina Faso* (The price of wives, the value of Guin women of Burkina Faso) (Paris: EHESS, Centre d'Etudes Africaines, 1990. 75p.); and Michele Dacher, 'Génies, ancêtres, voisins: quelques aspects de la relation à la terre chez les Ciranba (Goin) du Burkina Faso' (Genies, ancestors, neighbours: some aspects of the relationship with the earth among the Ciranba (Guin) of Burkina Faso), *Cahiers d'Etudes Africaines* (Paris), vol. 24, no. 2 (1984), p. 157-92.

# The Bisa

113 **Le regard du serpent: réflexions sur la théorie de la contamination chez les Bisa de Haute-Volta.** (The eye of the snake: reflections on the theory of contamination among the Bisa of Upper Volta.)
Sylvie Fainzang. *L'Homme* (Paris), vol. 24, no. 3/4 (July-Dec. 1984), p. 23-64.

A discussion of Bisa concepts of illness and traditional medicine. Among the Bisa contamination is perceived in terms of its meaning and the conditions under which it occurs, calling for both natural and supernatural cures. For more on this theme, see Sylvie Fainzang (et al.), *L'intérieur des choses: maladie, divination et reproduction sociale chez les Bisa du Burkina* (The inside of things: illness, divination and social reproduction among the Bisa of Burkina) (Paris: Harmattan, 1986. 204p. maps). For a more general anthropological analysis of the Bisa, see Jean Bernard, *Les Bisa du cercle de Garango* (The Bisa of the Garango circle) (Paris: CNRS, 1966. 252p.) and Odette P. Pegard, 'Structures et relations sociales en pays Bisa' (Social structures and relationships in Bisa country), *Cahiers d'Etudes Africaines* (Paris), vol. 5, no. 2 (1965), p. 161-247.

114 **Les sexes et leurs nombres: sens et fonction du 3 et du 4 dans une société burkinabe.** (The sexes and their numbers: the meaning and function of numbers 3 and 4 in a Burkinabe society.)
Sylvie Fainzang. *L'Homme* (Paris), vol. 25, no. 96 (1985), p. 97-109.

The author analyses in sociological terms the widespread African tendency to associate the numbers three and four with man and woman respectively, an association attributed to aspects of their anatomy. Using the example of the Bisa she suggests that symbolism serves to establish social relationships based on male domination.

# The Gurunsi

115  **Interprétation de la maladie chez les Winyé, Gurunsi du Burkina Faso: critique d'une théorie de la contamination.** (Interpretation of illness among the Gurunsi Winye: a critique of a theory of contamination.)
Jean-Pierre Jacob. *Genève-Afrique* (Geneva), vol. 25, no. 1 (1987), p. 59-88. map. bibliog.
A multifaceted analysis (including an English summary) of explanations given for illnesses by the Gurunsi. The author rejects Western notions of medical anthropology such as contagion and contamination which he feels do not correspond to all local conditions and perceptions of the causes of illness that include sorcery and spirit possession.

116  **Le totalitarisme élémentaire.** (Basic totalitarianism.)
Maurice Duval. *Cahiers Internationaux de Sociologie* (Paris), no. 84 (1988), p. 71-83.
An expansion on the author's classic book (see item no. 117), arguing that totalitarianism is not necessarily solely the function of state omnipotence in social, economic and political matters. It may manifest itself in much more elementary lineage-based societies such as those of Burkina Faso, where fear and anguish caused by sorcery can be exploited by giving the populace an antidote – worship of the Kwere (Chief). For an account of Gurunsi sacred chiefs, see Kunz Dittmer, *Sakralen Häuptlinge der Gurunsi im Ober-Volta* (Sacred chiefs of the Gurunsi in Upper Volta) (Hamburg, Germany: De Bruyter, 1961. 176p.).

117  **Un totalitarisme sans état. Essai d'anthropologie politique à partir d'un village burkinabe.** (Totalitarianism without a state: an essay on political anthropology based on a Burkinabe village.)
Maurice Duval. Paris: Harmattan, 1985. 183p.
A much-acclaimed path-breaking anthropological study based on research among the Nuna (closely related to the Gurunsi) in southern central Burkina Faso. The author illustrates the degree to which acute repression and social fear can exist without the existence of a central state apparatus – in this case through social domination by lineage-group heads and widespread fear of witchcraft and sorcery.

# The Gurma

118 **La calebasse de l'excision en pays gourmantche.** (The excision calabash in Gurma country.)
Michel Cartry. *Journal de la Société des Africanistes* (Paris), vol. 38, no. 2 (1968), p. 189-225.
A detailed outline of initiation rites among Gurma clans in the Diapoga region, required of all girls about to marry and join their husband's household. These include five-week cliteridectomy rites.

119 **From the village to the bush: an essay on the Gourmantche of Gobnangou.**
Michel Cartry. In: *Between belief and transgression*, edited by Michel Izard, Pierre Smith Chicago, Illinois: University of Chicago Press, 1982, p. 210-28.
Cartry outlines Gurma traditional beliefs, set against the duality of the village context that provides safety, and the bush, where danger prevails. Especially notable among Cartry's many articles on the Gurma is 'Attitudes familiales chez les Gourmantche' (Family attitudes among the Gurma), *L'Homme* (Paris), vol. 6, no. 3 (July-Sept. 1966), p. 41-67; 'Clans, lignages et groupements familiaux chez les Gourmantche de la région de Diapaga' (Clans, lineages and family groups among the Gurma of the Diapaga region), *L'Homme* (Paris), vol. 6, no. 2 (April-June 1966), p. 53-81.

120 **Gourmantche ethnoanthropology: a theory of human being.**
Richard Alan Swanson. Lanham, Maryland: University Press of America, 1985. 464p. maps. bibliog.
This major work povides comprehensive coverage of Gurma philosophy and religion, including texts in the Gurma language.

121 **Le suaire du chef.** (The chief's shroud.)
Michel Cartry. In: *Sous le masque de l'animal: essais sur le sacrifice en Afrique Noire*, edited by Michel Cartry. Paris: Presses Universitaires de France, 1987, p. 131-231. map. bibliog.
A study of the rôle of sacrifices during chiefly successions among the Gurma of Burkina Faso. Sacrifices serve a number of purposes: to assuage the spirits, to honour the deceased chief, and to assure the continued support of ancestors for the new chief. The author identifies the precise timing and sequence of the sacrifices, and the preferred offering in each instance. Some of this material can also be found in the author's three-part contribution 'Le statut de l'animal dans le système sacrificiel des Gourmantche' (The status of the animal in the sacrificial system of the Gurma), *Systèmes de Pensée en Afrique Noire* (Paris), no. 2 (1976), p. 141-75; no. 3 (1978), p. 17-58; no. 5 (1981), p. 195-216.

# The Nyonyosi

122  **Kinkirsi, Boghoba, Saba: das Weltbild der Nyonyosi in Burkina Faso.**
(Kinkirsi, Boghoba, Saba: the conception of the world of the Nyonyosi
of Burkina Faso.)
Anne-Marie Schweeger-Hefel. Vienna: A. Schendl, 1986. 436p. map.
A massive study, by the foremost scholar of Burkina Faso, of the cosmology and world
philosophy of the Nyonyosi, who are close to the Mossi. The complex, much-acclaimed
work includes numerous photographs of traditional ceremonies. An equally comprehensive work on the rôle of masks (including 130 plates) and social myths in
Nyonyosi and Silomsi society is *Masken und Mythen, Sozialstrukturen der Nyonyosi
und Silomse in Obervolta* (Masks and myths: social structure of the Nyonyosi and
Silomse of Upper Volta) (Vienna: A. Schendl, 1980. 480p.).

**Haut-Sénégal–Niger.** (Upper Senegal–Niger)
*See* item no. 5.

**Kokona. Essai d'histoire structurale.** (Kokona. Essay on structural history.)
*See* item no. 41.

**La légende royale des Kouroumba.** (The royal legend of the Kurumba.)
*See* item no. 42.

**L'Empire du Mogho-Naba.** (The Mogho-Naba Empire.)
*See* item no. 52.

**Gens de pouvoir, gens de terre.** (People of power, people of the earth.)
*See* item no. 55.

**The Mossi Kingdoms.**
*See* item no. 61.

**The Mossi of Burkina Faso.**
*See* item no. 62.

**Kunst und Religion der Lobi.** (Art and religion of the Lobi.)
*See* item no. 351.

# Labour and Labour Migrations

123 **L'autre Abidjan: chronique d'un quartier oublié.** (The other Abidjan: chronicles of a forgotten quarter.)
Alain Bonnassieux. Paris: Karthala, 1987. 220p. maps. bibliog.
A sociological study of Vridi-Canal, one of the oldest peripheral quarters of Abidjan. There are large numbers of Mossi among the polyglot population of non-nationals. The author describes the rich daily life of petty trade, commerce and artisan work in the quarter, and the changing relationships between the various groups found within it – their status changes according to their year of arrival – and their efforts to become integrated in the socio-economic life of Abidjan proper.

124 **Caractéristiques des migrations et de la nuptialité en pays lobi dagara.** (Characteristics of migration and marriage in Lobi Dagara areas.)
D. Benoît, P. Lévi, M. Pilon. Paris: ORSTOM, 1986. 161p. bibliog.
A study of patterns of migration, marriage practices, and levels of fertility in regions inhabited by the Lobi Dagara in southwest Burkina Faso. The work, supported by numerous statistical tables, reveals an out-migration to Ghana and Côte d'Ivoire, (small compared to that in Mossi regions), by young single males who are absent for an average period of four years. For more material on Lobi migration to Côte d'Ivoire, see Michele Fieloux, *Les sentiers de la nuit: les migrations rurales lobi de la Haute-Volta vers la Côte d'Ivoire* (Paths in the night: Lobi rural migration from Upper Volta towards Côte d'Ivoire) (Paris: ORSTOM, 1980. 199p. maps. bibliog.).

125 **Children of the *zongo*: the transformation of ethnic identities in Ghana.**
Enid Schildkrout. New York: Cambridge University Press, 1978. 303p. bibliog.
A study of the *zongo* (strangers' quarter) of Kumasi, Ghana, and the acculturation processes there. Among the groups in the *zongo* there are large numbers of Mossi, working on nearby farms. The book, written by the Assistant Curator of the American Museum of Natural History, focuses on their occupations, social hierarchy, customs and marriage patterns, and relationships with other ethnic groups in the *zongo* and

outside it. The study is directly comparable to that of Alain Bonnassieux (see item no. 123) on the Mossi in Abidjan.

126    **Contribution à l'étude du phénomène migratoire et de la condition juridique des étrangers en Haute-Volta.** (Contribution to the study of the migratory phenomenon and the legal position of strangers in Upper Volta.)
Cheikh Ouedraogo. *Revue Juridique et Politique* (Paris), vol. 34, no. 1 (Jan.-March 1980), p. 109-20.
Written by the chief magistrate of Ouagadougou, this article outlines migrant labour law in Burkina Faso which recognizes the rights of those who have left the country, and assures their protection abroad through bilateral treaties with neighbouring countries.

127    **Creating hunger: labor and agricultural policies in southern Mossi, 1919-1940.**
Raymond Gervais. In: *African population and capitalism: historical perspectives*, edited by D. D. Cordell, J. W. Gregory. Boulder, Colorado: Westview Press, 1987, p. 109-21.
A terse analysis of the effect on Mossi agriculture of early colonial policies favouring coastal colonies. One result was massive labour outflows from insular Burkina Faso which persist to this day. Compounded by poor soils and climate conditions, the effect has been to pauperize one of Africa's best-structured kingdoms.

128    **De la savane à la ville: essai sur la migration mossi vers Abidjan et sa région.** (From the savannah to the town: Mossi migration to Abidjan and its region.)
Raymond Deniel. Paris: Aubier-Montaigne, 1968. 223p. bibliog.
This is one of the first works to utilize survey analysis in assessing Mossi migration to Abidjan, supplemented by interviews in a specific Yatenga village found to have sent disproportionately large numbers of workers to Côte d'Ivoire. The author traces the roots of Voltaic out-migration to the colonial era's forced labour and high local taxes that drove Mossi to seek better-paying opportunities abroad.

129    **De quelques caractéristiques de la pratique matrimoniale Mossi contemporaine.** (On several characteristics of marriage practice among contemporary Mossi.)
J. Capron, J. M. Kohler. In: *Marriage, fertility and parenthood in West Africa*, edited by C. Oppong (et al.). Canberra: Australian National University Press, 1978, p. 187-223.
Utilizing statistical data, the authors examine the relationship between marriage practices and out-migration in Mossi areas. The monopoly exercised by traditional chiefs over matrimonial networks results in self-allocation of many wives, their denial to younger males, and a scarcity of women, reinforcing migration for purposes of accumulation of wealth and bride-price. Slowly eroded by modern marriage practices of Mossi fathers, this factor still has some effect.

Labour and Labour Migrations

130 **Employment opportunity and migration among the Mossi of Upper Volta.**
Gregory A. Finnegan. *Research in Economic Anthropology* (Greenwich, Connecticut), vol. 3 (1980), p. 291-322.

The available literature on Mossi migrations to neighbouring territories is critically examined in this work. The author maintains that the data used for most research do not take into account the facts of socio-economic change, and that recent data, not fully assessed, would show that Mossi out-migration is motivated by more varied reasons.

131 **Formation de la classe ouvrière en Afrique Noire: l'exemple du Burkina Faso.** (Formation of a working class in Black Africa: the example of Burkina Faso.)
Jean-Bernard Ouedraogo. Paris: Harmattan, 1989. 207p. bibliog.

A case-study of the sugar workers on the plantations of the Société Sucrière de Haute-Volta, the stratification and politicization of labour, their conditions of work and demands.

132 **Labour migration among the Mossi of the Upper Volta.**
Elliott Percival Skinner. In: *Urbanization and migration in West Africa*, edited by Hilda Kuper. Westport, Connecticut: Greenwood Press, 1981, p. 60-84.

A reprint of an edition issued in 1965 (University of California Press), this is a survey of the seasonal labour migration of Mossi to the plantations and mines of Ghana and Côte d'Ivoire, and to Benin and Mali. See also the author's 'Labour migration and its relationship to socio-cultural change in Mossi society' *Africa* (London), vol. 30, no. 2 (Oct. 1960), p. 375-401; and Victor D. Du Bois's two reports: 'Ahmadou's world: a case-study of a Voltaic immigrant to Ivory Coast', *American Field Staff Reports* (Hanover, New Hampshire), West Africa series, vol. 8, no. 2 (1965), p. 63-76, and 'The economic, social and political implications of Voltaic migration to Ivory Coast', *American Field Staff Reports.* vol. 14, no. 1 (1972), p. 1-9.

133 **Mass immigration from Upper Volta: the facts and implications.**
Ambroise Songre. *International Labour Review* (Geneva), (Aug.-Sept. 1973), p. 209-25.

Voltaic immigration has repercussions both for Burkina Faso and the countries in which the migrants settle. After discussing the historical context and dimensions of the migration, the author concludes that migration is a necessary evil but should be more tightly controlled and monitored by both bilateral and multilateral agreements.

134 **Mesures gouvernementales et/ou intérêts divergents des pays
exporteurs de main d'oeuvre et de pays hôtes: Haute-Volta et Côte
d'Ivoire.** (Divergence of interests between labour-exporting and host
countries, and measures taken by them: Upper Volta and Côte
d'Ivoire.)
Raymond Deniel. In: *Modern migrations in Western Africa*, edited by
Samir Amin. London: Oxford University Press, 1974, p. 215-25.
Starting as forced labour for the construction of the Abidjan–Bobo Dioulassou railway,
the abolition of corvée labour saw Ivorien employers organize recruitment services in
Upper Volta to attract Voltaic labour. These unregulated activities were abolished by
Ouagadougou after independence, to be replaced by a treaty between the two
countries spelling out mutual obligations regarding migrant labour. Mutual acrimony
has been ceaseless, with some treaty provisions ignored by Burkina Faso, while Côte
d'Ivoire has continued low levels of compensation, following a policy of localization
that penalizes Voltaic manpower.

135 **Migration in Upper Volta.**
Julien Conde. In: *Demographic aspects of migration in West Africa*,
edited by K. C. Zacharia, N. K. Nair. Washington, DC: The World
Bank, 1980, vol. 2, p. U.V. 1-156. maps. (Staff Working Paper, no.
415).
An analysis of population migration into Burkina Faso, based on data relating to 1960
and 1970, aided by maps and tables that give, in minute detail the age distribution,
occupation, sex, locality and country of origin of Burkina Faso's foreign migrant
workers.

136 **Migrations, société et développement en pays Mossi.** (Migration, society
and development in Mossi country.)
Gilles Sautter. *Cahiers d'Etudes Africaines* (Paris), vol. 20, no. 3
(1980), p. 215-53. maps. bibliog.
Research in Mossi regions indicates that migration patterns and motivations are
complex, resulting in manpower outflows to Ghana and Côte d'Ivoire but also
domestic rural–urban and rural–rural migrations. Demographic factors are not the sole
ones triggering the migrations: kinship/lineage disputes are also important, although
not the quest for bride-wealth, stressed in other accounts. The fact that internal
migration to free land elsewhere is more important than has been assumed hitherto,
requires the government to organize this manpower movement rather than let it
proceed haphazardly. For a study of Fulani migration patterns, see Michel Benoit,
'Pastoralisme et migration: les Peuls de Barani et de Dokue' (Pastoralism and
migration: the Fulani of Barani and Dokue), *Etudes Rurales* (Paris), no. 70 (April-
June 1978), p. 9-49.

137 **Migrations as revolt: the example of the Ivory Coast and Upper Volta
before 1945.**
A. I. Asiwaju. *Journal of African History* (Cambridge), vol. 17, no. 4
(1976), p. 577-94.
A survey of politically motivated manpower migrations which result from wide
divergences between political conditions in contiguous colonial territories. Such

'protest migrations constituted an important dimension of a series of unarmed but effective expressions of resentment by Africans against the European colonial presence' (p. 578). Asiwaju focuses on the out-migration from the Ivory Coast (which included the bulk of Upper Volta between 1932 and 1947) to the British-ruled Gold Coast, triggered by the more onerous French colonial system.

138   **Le mouvement coopératif en Haute-Volta.** (The cooperative movement in Upper Volta.)
      Gabriel Gosselin.   *Genève-Afrique* (Geneva), vol. 8, no. 1 (1969), p. 19-33.

This is an early survey on the development of Upper Volta's cooperatives since the decree of 1955 which permitted their creation.

139   **Un pouvoir des travailleurs peut-il être contre syndicats?** (Can workers' power work against the trade unions?)
      Charles Kabéya Muasé.   *Politique Africaine* (Paris), no. 33 (1989), p. 50-8.

An overview (including an English summary) of the relations between the country's unions and the populist régime of Thomas Sankara. Having achieved power with considerable unionist support, Sankara's CNR [Conseil National pour la Révolution] suppressed trade unions in Burkina Faso, arguing that his régime better represented the totality of labour in the country.

140   **Régime foncier et migrations: l'expérience de l'Aménagement des Vallées des Volta.** (System of land tenure and migration: the land development experiment of the Volta Valleys Authority.)
      D. B. Sidibe.   In: *Espaces disputés en Afrique noire*, edited by B. Crousse (et al.).   Paris: Karthala, 1986, p. 187-98.

A survey (which includes an English summary) of the problems experienced in settling new farm manpower in regions freed of endemic onchocercosis. The re-settlement scheme is run by the World Health Organization (WHO) and administered by the Volta Valleys Authority. Hostility and friction with existing farmers in the area has been intense, with the government timid in supporting new settlers. For another study of internal migrations see Jean-Paul Lahuec, Jean-Yves Marchal, *La mobilité du peuplement Bissa et Mossi* (The movements of Bissa and Mossi peoples) (Paris, ORSTOM, 1979. 149p. maps. bibliog.).

141   **Les salariés du Burkina: faut-il parler des classes moyennes?** (Salaried workers in Burkina Faso: can they be seen as the middle class?)
      J. M. Derrien.   *Tiers Monde* (Paris) vol. 26, no. 10 (Jan.-March 1985), p. 69-78.

An assessment of Burkinabe salaried labour that, according to the author, cannot be seen as the country's middle class. Only small numbers meet the criteria of a middle class; these include the financial, industrial and commercial élites, administrators, politicians and the upper echelons of the salaried workers, with the army keeping an equilibrium among the different segments of the privileged groups.

142 **Syndicalisme et démocratie en Afrique noire: l'expérience du Burkina Faso (1936-1988).** (Syndicalism and democracy in Black Africa: the experience of Burkina Faso 1936-88.)
Charles Kabéya Muasé. Paris: Karthala, 1989. 252p. map. bibliog.

Organized labour has played a crucial rôle in several coups and attempted coups, starting with the strikes that helped topple the First Republic of President Maurice Yaméogo. This book is the first comprehensive study of Burkinabe unionism, and because trade unions have been so important, this is in many ways also a political history of Burkina Faso itself. The author retraces the history of organized labour, its constant tug-of-war with whatever régime has been in power and the current delicate balance of power between Campaore and Burkinabe labour. The book is a condensed version of the author's 1988 dissertation. An even more abridged version appeared as Charles Kabéya Muasé, 'Evolution et rôle des syndicats au Burkina Faso' (The evolution and rôle of unions in Burkina Faso), *Présence Africaine* (Paris), no. 142, (1987), p. 130-47.

143 **Underdevelopment, dependence and migration in Upper Volta.**
Joel W. Gregory. In: *The politics of Africa, dependence and development*, edited by Timothy Shaw, Kenneth A. Heard. London: Longman, 1979, p. 73-94.

An outline of patterns of rural migration by the foremost scholar writing in English on this subject. There were three phases: during the colonial era, migration was a result of the country's colonial status; after the end of the Second World War, a symptom of the territory's underdevelopment compared to Côte d'Ivoire, fuelled by a history of prior out migration; and following independence, when an influx from outlying regions into a swollen Ouagadougou meant that the city competed 'with Ghana and Ivory Coast as destinations for migration' (p. 89). See also the author's 'Development and in-migration in Upper Volta', in *Modern migrations in Western Africa*, edited by Samir Amin (London: Oxford University Press, 1974, p. 305-20); and 'Urbanization and development planning in Upper Volta: the education variable?' in *Urbanization, national development and regional planning in Africa*, edited by Robert A. Obudho, Salah S. A. Shackhs (New York: Praeger, 1974, p. 130-42). The latter stresses that rural migration results from unequal rates of economic growth in the country, to be averted by a stress on providing rural schools and facilities within the context of a rurally oriented developmental strategy.

# Languages and Linguistics

144 **Les bwamu et ses dialectes.** (Bwamu and its dialects.)
Gabriel Manessy. *Bulletin d'IFAN* (Dakar), vol. 23, no. 1-2 (Jan.-
April 1961), p. 119-78.
A study of Bwamu and its several dialects.

145 **Contribution à l'etude des langues voltaïques.** (Contribution to the study
of the Voltaic languages.)
André Prost. Dakar: IFAN, 1964. 461p.
The classic survey of Burkina Faso's main languages by the linguist priest who served
in various capacities in several countries in West Africa. See also Norbert Nikiéma, *La
situation linguistique en Haute-Volta* (The linguistic situation in Upper Volta) (Paris:
UNESCO, 1980).

146 **Dictionnaire bobo–français, précédé d'une introduction grammaticale et
suivi d'un lexique français–bobo.** (Bobo–French dictionary, preceded by
a grammar introduction, and followed by a French–Bobo lexicon.)
Pierre Le Bris, André Prost. Paris: SELAF, 1981. 415p.
French–Bobo dictionary and linguistic study (through an examination of proverbs) by
two of France's foremost linguists. An English summary is included.

147 **Dictionnaire encyclopédique moore–français.** (Encyclopaedic
More–French dictionary.)
Jean Bigtarma Zaongo. Ouagadougou: Zaongo, 1985. 3 vols.
A comprehensive More–French dictionary.

148 **Dictionnaire koromfa.** (Koromfa dictionary.)
John R. Rennison. Hamburg, Germany: H. Buske, 1986. 276p.
A French–Koromfa dictionary.

149 **Esquisse du système grammatical Lobi.** (Outline of Lobi grammar.)
Charles Lamothe. Paris: CNRS, 1967, 188p.
An outline of Lobi grammar at a fairly basic linguistic level.

150 **Etudes gulmances: phonologie, classes nominales, lexique.** (Gulmance
studies: phonology, noun classes, lexicon.)
Bernard Surugue. Paris: SELAF, 148p. bibliog.
A linguistic and grammatical study of Gulmance, one of the Gurma languages. The
work includes a brief Gulmance–French dictionary as well as an English summary. See
also Michael Kenstowicz (et al.), 'Tonal polarity in two Gur languages', *Studies in
Linguistic Sciences* (Urbana, Illinois), vol. 18, no. 1 (1988), p. 77-103; Annie Rialland,
'Le système tonal du gurma, langue gur de Haute-Volta' (The tonal system of Gurma,
a Gur language in Upper Volta), *Journal of African Languages and Linguistics*
(Dordrecht, The Netherlands), vol. 3, no. 1 (1981), p. 39-64.

151 **A Fulfulde–English dictionary.**
I. A. Mukosy. Kaduna, Nigeria: Nigerian Educational and
Development Council, 1991. 220p.
A Fulani–English dictionary.

152 **Le Kusaal.** (Kusaal.)
André Prost. Dakar: Université de Dakar, Département de
Linguistique Générale, 1979. 167p.
Important linguistic study of the language of the Kusaase found in Burkina Faso and
Ghana. See also the author's *Le Viémo* (Dakar: Université de Dakar, Département de
Linguistique Générale, 1979. 86p.), which is the only linguistic study in any language
of the small ethnic group of the same name.

153 **La langue des Kouroumba ou Akurumfé.** (The Kurumba language or
Akurumfe.)
André Prost. Vienna: A. Schendl, 1980. 179p. bibliog.
A pioneering study of the Koromfa language of the Kurumba of north Burkina Faso.
He is one of the most respected linguists of the Voltaic languages.

154 **La langue more: dialecte de Ouagadougou.** (The More language: the
Ouagadougou dialect.)
Gaston Canu. Paris: SELAF, 1976. 421p. bibliog.
An important linguistic study of the More language, including a summary in English.
Phonetic and lexical differences among the four dialects of Ouagadougou, Ouahigouya,
Kaya and Tenkodogo are noted. For an earlier seminal work, see Pierre G. Alexandre,
*La langue more* (The More language) (Dakar: IFAN, 1953. 2 vols).

155 **Langues du Burkina Faso.** (Languages of Burkina Faso.)
G. Kédrébéogo, Z. Yaga. Ouagadougou: Ministère de
l'Enseignement Supérieur et de la Recherche Scientifique, 1986. 57p.
bibliog.

A linguistic study of the Gurunsi languages spoken by 600,000 people in Burkina Faso, Togo and Ghana. The bulk of the work is composed of a dictionary of common words as they appear in eight Gurunsi dialects.

156 **Les langues Gurunsi.** (The Gurunsi languages.)
Gabriel Manessy. Paris: SELAF, 1969. 2 vols.

This linguistic and grammatical study describes the various Gurunsi languages.

157 **Les langues Oti-Volta: classification généalogique d'un groupe de
langues voltaïques.** (The Oti-Volta languages: genealogical classification
of a group of Voltaic languages.)
Gabriel Manessy. Paris: SELAF, 1975. 314p. map. bibliog.

The Gur languages, formerly divided into the Gurunsi and the Oti-Volta groups, are spoken in eastern central Burkina Faso and in neighbouring countries to the south. Together with Koromfa (language of the Kurumba) they are all derived from what the author calls the 'proto-central' language. Several conjectures are formulated regarding the geographical location of this original community, and the histories of the groups issuing from it. An English summary is provided.

158 **Lexical phonology and morphology: the nominal classes in Fula.**
Carole Paradis. New York: Garland, 1992. 313p. bibliog.

The lexical phonology, morphology and grammar of the Fulani language are described in this work. For two other grammars of Fula, see Mary McIntosh, *Fulfulde syntax and verbal morphology* (Boston, Massachusetts: KP & Ibadan University Press, 1984. 292p.); and D. W. Arnott, *The nominal and verbal system of Fula* (Oxford: Clarendon Press, 1970. 432p.).

159 **Manuel de langue peule: dialecte du Liptako.** (Manual of the Fulani
language, Liptako dialect.)
Lucien Bidaud, André Prost. Paris: Publications Orientalistes de
France, 1982. 236p. bibliog.

A manual of the 'practical' Fulani grammar and syntax of the Liptako dialect centred around Dori. For a pioneering work on Fula, see Henri Labouret, *La langue des Peuls ou Fulbe* (The Fulani language or Fulbe) (Dakar: IFAN, 1952. 286p.).

160 **More, basic course.**
Marianne Lehr, James E. Redden, Adama Balima. Washington, DC:
US Government Printing Office, 1966. 340p.

Part of the Department of State's Foreign Service Institute 'Basic Courses', this is the only easily available English textbook of More language instruction. The manual is composed of three sections aimed at progressive mastery of the language, from basic socially useful expressions to advanced conversational skills. An equivalent in French is Norbert Nikiéma, *Ed gom moore: la grammaire du moore en 50 leçons* (Ed gom moore: More grammar in fifty lessons) (Ouagadougou: University of Ouagadougou, 1980. 2 vols). Another classic text is Leo Frobenius, *Manuel pratique de langue More* (Practical handbook of the More language) (Paris: Fournier, 1923. 326p.).

161 **Un morphème de classe supplémentaire en fulfulde, dialect Jelgooji, Haute-Volta.** (The morpheme of an extra category in Fulfulde, Jelgooji dialect, Upper Volta.)
René Vellette. *Journal of West African Languages* (Cambridge, England), vol. 15, no. 1 (April 1985), p. 93-103.
This work deals with morphophonology, consonant alternation and nominals in Fulani. See also the author's 'La focalisation en fulfulde' (Focalization in Fulfulde), *Journal of West African Languages* (Dallas), vol. 18, no. 2 (1988), p. 9-20.

162 **Prédication et énonciation en kasim.** (Preaching and articulation in Kasim.)
Emilio Bonvini. Paris: CNRS, 1988. 198p.
Linguistic study of the Kasim language, spoken by some 120,000 people in southern Burkina Faso. See also the author's 'La bouche: entre la parole et l'insulte: l'example du Kasim' (The mouth: between words and insults), *Journal des Africanistes* (Paris), vol. 57, no. 1-2 (1987), p. 149-59. For a phonology and morphology of the language see William J. Greenspan, 'Metathesis in Kasem' in *Phonology in the 1980's*, edited by Didier L. Goyvaerts (Ghent, Belgium: Story-Scientia, 1981, p. 101-18); Annie Rialland, 'Y a-t-il vraiment des metathèses en kasem?' (Are there really metatheses in Kasem?), *Afrique et Langage* (Paris), vol. 25 (1986), p. 5-34. See also A. K. Awedoba, 'The status of preverbal items in Kasem', *Afrika und Ubersee* (Hamburg), vol. 72, no. 1 (1989), p. 191-209.

163 **Systématique du significant en Dagara: variété Wule.** (Systemization of the signifier in Dagara: Wule dialect.)
Penou-Achille Some. Paris: Harmattan, 1982. 491p. maps.
The phonology of the Wule Lobi dialect is described in detail in this study. See also Alain Delplanque, 'Les verbes de jugement en dagara' (Verbs of judgement in Dagara), *Journal des Africanistes* (Paris), vol. 57, no. 1-2 (1987), p. 133-47.

164 **Textes koromfés.** (Koromfe texts.)
John R. Rennison, Wilhelm Staude. Hamburg, Germany: H. Buske, 1986, 125p.
Texts in Koromfa and in French translation are reprinted as an aid to mastery of the language.

165 **Die verhinderte Mitsprache: Aspekte zur Sprachpolitik in Ghana, Togo und Obervolta.** (Prevented speech: aspects of language policy in Ghana, Togo and Upper Volta.)
Gunther Rusch. Hamburg, Germany: Institut für Afrika-Kunde, 1984. 214p. bibliog.
A comparative study of the languages and language policy in Ghana, Togo and Burkina Faso. An English-language summary is included.

**Haut-Sénégal–Niger.** (High Senegal–Niger.)
*See* item no. 5.

**Les tribus du rameau Lobi.** (The tribes of the Lobi wedge.)
*See* item no. 92.

# Religion

166 **An eye in the sky, one deep in the earth: elements of Zaose religion.**
Allen Roberts.   In: *Ethnologies: hommage à Marcel Griaule*,
edited by Solange Ganay (et al.).   Paris: Hermann, 1987, p. 291-306.
A survey of the religious beliefs of the Zaose, a group who are closely related to the
Mossi. Notwithstanding the adoption of modern religions, to this day many aspects of
traditional Zaose beliefs and rites are kept alive by chiefs and commoners alike. Zaose
migrant workers continue to sacrifice a fowl and collect a stone at a sacred shrine on
their way to Côte d'Ivoire or Ghana, as a protection against evil spirits.

167 **Approche de la religion des Birifor.** (Approach to the religion of the
Birifor.)
Alfred Erbs.   Paris: Musée de l'Homme, 1975. 75p. map.
An ouline of the customs, cosmology and religious beliefs of the Birifor, including their
feast-days, death and purification rites, and the rôle of sacrifices. For a survey of Guin
witchcraft practices see Michele Dacher, 'De l'origine et de la nature des tinni goin'
(On the origins and nature of the tinni goin), *Systèmes de Pensée en Afrique Noire*
(Paris), vol. 8 (1985), p. 69-109.

168 **Christianity and Islam among the Mossi.**
Elliott Percival Skinner.   *American Anthropologist* (Monasha,
Wisconsin), vol. 60, no. 6 (Dec. 1958). p. 1102-19.
A study of the rapid spread of Islam among the Mossi despite the early arrival of
Christian missions with the onset of the colonial era. Skinner lists the attractive aspects
of Islam (adaptability to local conditions and simplicity of doctrine) in contrast to
Christianity which is perceived as the conqueror's religion, with its rejection of strongly
ingrained indigenous cultural norms, and its association with forced labour under the
French. For the traditional religious practices of the Mossi, see also Pierre Ilboudo,
*Croyances et pratiques religieuses traditionnelles des Mossi* (Beliefs and traditional
religious practices of the Mossi) (Paris: CNRS, 1966. 109p. bibliog).

47

## Religion

169 **La crise de la communauté musulmane de Haute-Volta.** (The crisis in the Muslim community of Upper Volta.)
René Otayek. *Cahiers d'Etudes Africaines* (Paris), vol. 24, no. 3 (1984), p. 299-320. bibliog.

An analysis of the ambiguous status of Islam in Burkina Faso. Although the dominant religion in number of believers, the faith occupies a subordinate rôle in society. Barely tolerated until independence, and since then gaining adherents mostly due to non-religious reasons, the community's internal divisions and inability to cope with the challenges of modernization have kept Islam out of much of the political élite, leading to a major crisis within Muslim organizations in 1983. For these internal schisms, see Assimi Kouanda, 'Les conflits au sein de la communauté musulmane du Burkina: 1962-1986' (Internal conflicts within the Muslim community in Burkina, 1962-1986), *Islam et Sociétés du Sud du Sahara* (Paris), vol. 3 (1989), p. 7-26.

170 **Croyances religieuses et vie quotidienne: Islam et Christianisme à Ouagadougou.** (Religious beliefs and daily life: Islam and Christianity in Ouagadougou.)
Raymond Deniel. Paris: CNRS, 1970. 360p. map. bibliog.

One of the first studies of religious beliefs to employ survey analysis for the collection of data. The emphasis of the work is on how respondents perceived themselves and other religions: whether they see a rôle for their faith in daily life, and to what extent religious affiliation affects daily life. The author concludes that religion plays a serious rôle in Ouagadougou life, but that the élite are still largely the product of Roman Catholic schools. See also Assimi Kouanda, 'La religion musulmane: facteur d'intégration ou d'identification ethnique. Le cas des yarsé du Burkina Faso' (The Muslim religion: factor for integration or ethnic identification. The case of the Yarse of Burkina Faso), in *Les ethnies ont une histoire*, edited by J. P. Chrétien, G. Prunier. (Paris: Karthala, 1989, p. 125-34).

171 **L'église en Haute-Volta.** (The Church in Upper Volta.)
Special Issue of *Vivante Afrique* (Namur, Belgium) (Dec. 1962). 60p.

This account of cultural and religious beliefs in Burkina Faso describes the proselytizing, educational and medical work of the Catholic missions. For the story of the White Fathers in the country, see Paul Baudu, *Vieil empire, jeune église* (Old empire, new church) (Paris: Editions La Savane, 1956. 283p.). For that of the Ouagadougou Congregation of Black Sisters, and the difficulties and motivations of new recruits, see Marie Le Roy Ladurie, 'Etude sur les vocations religieuses au pays Mossi' (Study of the religious vocations in Mossi country), *Cahiers d'Etudes Africaines* (Paris), vol. 4, no. 14 (1963), p. 275-316. For the biography of one medical missionary resident in the country for forty years, see Roger de Benoist, *Docteur Lumière: quarante ans au service de l'homme en Haute Volta* (Dr. Lumière: forty years of service to man in Upper Volta) (Paris: Editions S.O.S., 1975. 236p.).

172 **L'état de la recherche sur l'Islam au Burkina.** (The state of research on Islam in Burkina Faso.)
Assimi Kouanda. *Islam et Sociétés du Sud du Sahara* (Paris), vol. 2 (1988), p. 94-105. bibliog.

In this survey of research on Islam in Burkina Faso, Kouanda notes that because of the historic Mossi rejection of Islam little attention was paid to the recent massive spread of that faith. The author states that more research is necessary now that the Islamic influence through mosques and Koranic schools is so visible throughout the country.

173  **L'Islam en Haute-Volta à l'époque coloniale.** (Islam in Upper Volta during the colonial era.)
Jean Audouin, Raymond Deniel.    Paris: Harmattan, 1978. 129p. maps. bibliog.

An examination of the rapid spread of Islam, a surprising feature since the region had strongly rejected Muslim influences in pre-colonial days. Not demanding a break with traditional, still-cherished animist practices, Islam's spread has been phenomenal. Between 1948 and 1955, for example, the number of Muslims in Ouagadougou doubled, while the Muslim Yatenga grew to sixty per cent. The authors explore the reason for these massive inroads, and analyse the country's main religious orders – qadriya, tidjaniya, and hamallism. For the immediate pre-colonial era, see H. Diallo, 'Introduction à l'étude de l'histoire de l'Islam dans l'ouest du Burkina Faso' (Introduction to the study of the history of Islam in west Burkina Faso), *Islam et Sociétés au Sud du Sahara* (Paris), vol. 4 (1990), p. 11-34.

174  **Islam in Mossi society.**
Elliott Percival Skinner.    In: *Islam in tropical Africa*, edited by I. M. Lewis.    London: Oxford University Press, 1969, p. 350-73.

Largely due to their strong political organization, the Mossi preserved their ethnic identity during the colonial era and efforts to convert them by force failed. However, mercantile contacts and the presence of Muslim merchants spread perceptions of the material advantages of such conversion, and the Mossi rapidly succumbed to Islam.

175  **Islam, sex roles and modernization in Bobo-Dioulasso.**
Lucy Quimby.    In: *The new religions of Africa*, edited by Benetta Jules-Rosette.    Norwood, New Jersey: Ablex Publishing, 1979. p. 203-218.

The cosmology and sex roles of the Dyula community of Bobo-Dioulasso are explored in this essay. Since most of the community refused to send their children to French schools during the colonial era, few Dyula attained posts in the emerging bureaucracy. On the other hand, the commercial growth of Bobo-Dioulasso from a small insignificant centre, loosened lineage solidarities and pitched men against women in the economic spheres. The spread of Islam not only changed cosmologies but also established patterns of behaviour, being used by males to claim their superiority in face of the growing asssertiveness of women.

176  **Les missionaires catholiques du Soudan Français et de la Haute Volta – entrepreneurs et formateurs d'artisans.** (The Catholic missionaries of French Sudan and Upper Volta: entrepreneurs and mentors of artisans.)
Joseph-Roger Benoist.    In: *Entreprises et entrepreneurs en Afrique*. Paris: Harmattan, 1983, p. 249-63.

The formative role of Catholic missions during the colonial era included the education of local people to become semi-skilled craftsmen and traders.

## Religion

177 **The position of women in the Sisala divination cult.**
Eugene L. Mendonsa. In: *The new religions of Africa*, edited by
Benetta Jules-Rosette. Norwood, New Jersey: Ablex Publishing,
1979, p. 57-66.
A study of the rôle of women in a divination cult among the Sisala in southern Burkina
Faso, where women are otherwise confined to a domestic rôle. The bulk of the article
describes the specific organization and forms of divination rites and cults in Sisala
villages. Women are allowed to play this one prominent ritual rôle in an otherwise
male-oriented society because it gives them no manipulative authority.

178 **Le pouvoir du Bangré: enquête initiatique à Ouagadougou.** (The power
of the Bangre: inquiry into initiation in Ouagadougou.)
Kabire Fidaali. Paris: Presses de la Renaissance, 1987. 220p. bibliog.
A study of shamanism and occult practices among the Mossi.

179 **The Quranic school farm and child labour in Upper Volta.**
Mahir Saul. *Africa* (London), vol. 52, no. 2 (1984), p. 71-87. bibliog.
An analysis of the reasons why farmers send their sons to Koranic schools where the
children have to work hard for their keep. The perceived benefits of this education
include being able to earn a salary through teaching others, and the social recognition
and spiritual satisfaction that ensues. Even acute poverty and insufficient household
grain as a result of the loss to the household of the child's labour are made acceptable
by such benefits.

180 **Sorciers, féticheurs et guérisseurs de la Côte d'Ivoire–Haute Volta.**
(Sorcerers, fetishists and healers of Côte d'Ivoire and Upper Volta.)
J. Kerharo, A. Bouquet. Paris: Vigot Frères, 1950. 144p. map.
A seminal examination of sorcery, witchcraft and fetishism, including the phar-
macological preparations (toxins) used in these activities. These authors also study
popular beliefs concerning the origins of diseases and reasons for death, the
administration of medical magic potions, and the manner in which infertility is treated
and aphrodisiacs are administered.

181 **Transgression, transversality, wandering.**
Michel Izard. In: *Between belief and transgression: structuralist essays
in religion, history and myth*, edited by Michel Izard, Pierre Smith.
Chicago, Illinois: University of Chicago Press, 1982, p. 229-44.
(Translated from *La fonction symbolique*. Paris: Gallimard, 1979).
A lucid overview, with examples, of the moral schism between social norms and
transgressions, including sexual deviance, among Yatenga's Mossi.

**Alfred Diban, premier chrétien de Haute-Volta.** (Alfred Diban, the first Christian of Upper Volta.)
*See* item no. 49.

**Islam et colonisation au Yatenga (1897-1950).** (Islam and the colonization of Yatenga, 1897-1950.)
*See* item no. 57.

# Gender Issues

182 **Beer, sorghum and women: production for the market in rural Upper Volta.**
Mahir Saul. *Africa* (London), vol. 51, no. 3 (1981), p. 746-64. map.
An attempt to draw attention to the considerable amount of trade, and profits, accruing to women involved in traditional commerce in a farming community 100 kilometres south of Ouagadougou. For the rôle of women as artisans, based on data from the 1970s, see S. A. Kambou (et al.), *L'artisanat féminin en Haute Volta* (Women's crafts in Upper Volta) (Ouagadougou: CVRS, 1978. 176p.).

183 **Le CNR et les femmes: de la difficulté de libérer 'la moitié du ciel'.** (The CNR and women: on the difficulties of liberating 'the other half'.)
Mathias S. Kanse. *Politique Africaine* (Paris), no. 33 (1989), p. 66-72.
An overview (with English summary) of ambiguities in the attitude of President Sankara's régime on the issue of female emancipation, and the resistance to change at all levels, including from traditional women themselves. See also Christine Benabdessadok. 'Femmes et révolution, ou comment libérer la moitié de la société' (Women and revolution, or how to free half of society), *Politique Africaine* (Paris), vol. 20 (1985), p. 54-64. For a more positive view of the rôle of women in revolutionary Burkina Faso, see G. Tarrab, C. Coenne, *Femmes et pouvoirs au Burkina Faso* (Women and power in Burkina Faso) (Paris: Harmattan, 1989. 125p.).

184 **Etat, patriarcat et développement: le cas d'un village du Burkina Faso.**
(State, patriarchalism and development: an example of a village in Burkina Faso.)
Brigitte Hannequin. *Canadian Journal of African Studies* (Toronto), vol. 24, no. 1 (1990), p. 36-49.
A study of the structure and operation of a village group set up in 1980 which indirectly perpetuates the tradition of patriarchal and male dominance in Mossi society.

185 **Etudes des mariages et divorces dans la ville de Ouagadougou 1980-83.**
(Studies on marriage and divorce in the town of Ouagadougou,
1980-83.)
Cecile Marie Zoungrana. Ouagadougou: Institut Nationale de la
Statistique et de la Démographie, 1986. 10p.
Interesting figures and data on formal marriage and divorce in Ouagadougou, where
traditional norms still predominate, are illustrated with tables and statistics. The data
indicate an average nine-year age-gap between male and female marriage partners
(women tend to marry at 20-21 years, men at 29-30) and a slow increase in modern
marriages [i.e. formally registered] and divorces during the period in question.

186 **Evasions féminines dans la Volta noire.** (Women's absconding in the
Black Volta.)
Anne Retel-Laurentin. *Cahiers d'Etudes Africaines* (Paris), vol. 19,
no. 1-4 (1979), p. 253-98.
An account of female adultery and desertion among the Bwa where marriage is viewed
as being irreversible. The disparity between customary law and reality, and the fact
that a wife's absconding is seen as a compliment to the aggrieved husband [because it
indicates excess virility], indicates there is a tacit acceptance by the community of the
duality of theory and reality. An English summary is included.

187 **Family planning in Burkina Faso: results of a survey.**
T. McGinn. *Studies in Family Planning* (New York), vol. 20, no. 6
(1989), p. 325-31.
A survey of women of reproductive age, investigating their knowledge of, attitudes
towards, and practice of contraception. The basic level of knowledge was found to be
surprisingly high, even though government family planning programmes had been
operating for only one year. However, only 4.9 per cent of women were using modern
methods of contraception, with forty-one per cent practising abstinence.

188 **Farm households in rural Burkina Faso: some evidence on allocative and
direct return to schooling and male–female labour productivity
differentials.**
Rati Ram, Ram D. Singh. *World Development* (Washington, DC),
vol. 16, no. 3 (1988), p. 419-24.
Using household data-sets, an assessment is made of the effect on productivity
produced by schooling, and of male–female productivity differentials in traditional
farming systems. The effect of schooling is modest, but the productivity of labour
inputs of women is much higher than that of men. For another survey of educational
returns, see George Psacharopoulus, 'Returns to education: a further international
update and implications', *Journal of Human Resources* (Madison, Wisconsin), vol. 20
(1985), p. 584-604.

## Gender Issues

189 **Femmes et groupements villageois au Burkina Faso.** (Women and village groups on Burkina Faso.)
Françoise Baulier. *Communautés* (Paris), no. 79 (Jan.-March 1987), p. 48-58.

An up-to-date inventory of women's groups involved in developmental tasks (some set up at the initiative of the Organization for Rural Development [ORD]) in five regions of Burkina Faso. For an in-depth analysis of one of these, funded by UNICEF, see Soon-Young Yoon, 'Le barrage des femmes: les femmes Mossi du Burkina Faso' (The women's barrage: Mossi women in Burkina Faso), *Tiers Monde* (Paris), vol. 26, no. 102 (1985), p. 443-9. For documentation of how even minor technological innovations can greatly ameliorate the daily life of women, see Grace S. Hemmings-Gapihan, 'Baseline study for socio-economic evaluation of Tangaye Solar site' in *Women and technological change in developing countries*, edited by Roslyn Dauber, Melinda L. Cain, (Boulder, Colorado: Westview Press, 1981, p. 139-48).

190 **Frauen der Lyela: die wirtschaftliche und soziale Lage der Frauen von Sanje, Burkina Faso.** (Lele women: the economic and social situation of women in Sanje.)
Sabine Steinbrich. Hohenschaftlarn bei Munich, Germany: K. Renner, 1987. 487p. maps. bibliog.

Comprehensive economic and social anthropological study of Lele women based on prolonged fieldwork in an area west of Koudougou. The work analyses all aspects of the rôle of women in society. Another useful book in German which surveys the rôle of women in rural development is Eva-Maria Bruchhaus, *Frauen in Obervolta* (Women in Upper Volta) (Freiburg im Breisgau, Germany: Arnold-Bergstraesser-Institut, 1979. 148p.).

191 **International development and the evolution of women's economic roles: a case study from northern Gulma, Upper Volta.**
Grace S. Hemmings-Gapihan. In: *Women and work in Africa*, edited by Edna G. Bay. Boulder, Colorado: Westview Press, 1982, p. 171-89. bibliog.

An outline of the changing socio-economic context in Burkina Faso which has eliminated the rôle of the extended family as a unit of production. Overpopulation has decreased the value of agricultural work in single-family plots, and forced out-migration as well as the quest for modern urban work by male family members. This in turn has raised the economically productive rôle of women in the agrarian sector to compensate for absentee males.

192 **Modernization, divorce and the status of women: le Tribunal Coutumier in Bobodioulasso.**
Carol Bohmer. *African Studies Review* (Waltham, Massachusetts), vol. 23, no. 2 (Sept. 1980), p. 81-90. bibliog.

A study of divorce law and practice in Burkina Faso's second-largest city, which dispels the conventional wisdom that modernization leads to an improvement in the status of women. An examination of the proceedings of the city's customary court (which handles both financial and family disputes), reveals that even when women have legal rights, these are often not enforced due to the perpetuation of customary practice.

193 **Paroles de femmes.** (Women's talk.)
Oger Kaboré. *Journal des Africanistes* (Paris), vol. 57, no. 1/2 (1987), p. 117-31.
Mossi describe the talk of women as dangerous and destructive, as opposed to that of men, which is seen as constructive and reasonable. Analysis reveals, however, that there is agreement that in certain contexts (reconciliation, education, and household management, for instance) women's intercession is much more effective. An English summary is included.

194 **The value of work-at-home and contributions of wives' household service in polygynous families.**
Ram D. Singh, Mathew J. Morey. *Economic Development and Cultural Change* (Chicago), vol. 35, no. 4 (1987), p. 743-65. bibliog.
Using cross-sectional household data, the authors estimate the productivity and income of farm-wives working at home in a variety of differing social and individual contexts. These range between $292 and $471 per annum, representing between 38 and 61 per cent of family farm incomes, a fact that underlines the significant economic contribution of Burkinabe women.

195 **Women's liberation and the African freedom struggle.**
Thomas Sankara. New York: Pathfinder Press, 1990, 36p. maps.
Two discourses by Burkina Faso's former charismatic leader, one on the occasion of International Women's Day 1987, and the second an extract from Sankara's Political Orientation Speech, that became the programme of the Burkinabe revolution.

**Islam, sex roles and modernization in Bobo-Dioulasso.**
*See* item no. 175.

**The position of women in the Sisala divination cult.**
*See* item no. 177.

**Le mariage en Haute-Volta.** (Marriage in Upper Volta.)
*See* item no. 264.

# Social Issues

196 **African urban life: the transformation of Ouagadougou.**
Elliott Percival Skinner.   Princeton, New Jersey: Princeton University
Press, 1974, 487p.

The classic analysis of life in Burkina Faso's capital from its foundation until the early
years of independence. All aspects are outlined: the city's physical setting; history;
traditional and modern economy; its political, social and religious institutions; and the
process of change taking place in all of these. The author, America's foremost scholar
of Burkina Faso, at the time chaired Columbia University's Anthropology department.

197 **Aménagement urbain et pratiques fonciers coutumières en Haute Volta.**
(Urban development and customary land practices in Upper Volta.)
J. M. Traore.   In: *Espaces disputés en Afrique noire*, edited by
Bernard Crousse, Emile Le Bris, Etienne Le Roy.   Paris: Karthala,
1986, p. 33-40.

Ouagadougou's annual growth rate of 7.5 per cent constitutes a grave problem for
urban planners. In 1984, assisted by the United Nations Development Programme
(UNDP), the World Bank and the Dutch government, legislation was passed aimed at
addressing the housing and land needs of low-income populations. In practice, the cost
of developing new land, and the need to set aside large tracts for 'customary owners'
has left the low-income group virtually unaffected. The book contains five other
contributions dealing with specific urban problems or village land-utilization issues
within Burkina Faso.

198 **Au sport, citoyens.** (To sports, citizens.)
Jean-Pierre Augustin, Yaya K. Drabo.   *Politique Africain*, no. 33
(1989), p. 59-65.

Outline of the CNR régime's comprehensive sports policy ideologically anchored in a
desire to produce a new citizenry which is both healthy and productive. Implementation of the policies espoused, however, has been constrained by a wide range of factors

that have tripped up similar efforts at mass involvement in other countries. An English summary is included.

199 **Bobo Dioulasso: le développement d'une ville d'Afrique occidentale.**
(Bobo Dioulasso: the development of a West African town.)
Yola Van Wettere-Verhasselt. *Cahiers d'Outre-mer* (Bordeaux),
vol. 22, no. 85 (Jan.-March 1969), p. 88-94.
A study of the growth and development of Burkina Faso's second-largest town, which at the time had 60,000 people.

200 **Burkina Faso: le secteur informel de Ouagadougou.** (Burkina Faso: the informal sector of Ouagadougou.)
Meine Pieter Van Dijk. Paris: Harmattan, 1986, 203p. bibliog.
Written by a Dutch economist at the Royal Tropical Institute in Amsterdam, the work examines what can be done to assist the 50-75 per cent of Ouagadougou's population who struggle for a livelihood in the informal sector. Based on empirical research in both Dakar (Senegal) and Ouagadougou, the author makes several proposals for implementation, and indeed formulates a new theory of informal markets.

201 **Démographies et villes au Burkina Faso.** (Demography of Burkina Faso cities.)
Pierre Sirven. *Cahiers d'Outre-mer* (Bordeaux), vol. 40, no. 159 (1987), p. 265-83.
A survey of the demographic prospects of Burkina Faso and its urban areas. As a virtual labour reserve of Ghana and Côte d'Ivoire, urbanization levels (12.5 per cent) are relatively low, but 67 per cent of the urban population is concentrated in only two towns and, if they continue to grow at current rates, it will pose massive urban problems including food shortages. There is an English summary.

202 **Les déterminants de la consommation urbaine à Ouagadougou.**
(Determinants of urban household consumption in Ouagadougou.)
Taladidia Thiombiano. *Africa Development* (Dakar), vol. 13, no. 2 (1988), p. 77-98. bibliog.
An empirical assessment of food consumption patterns in Ouagadougou households, in order to explain the paradox of heavy and costly imports of cereals when cheaper local varieties are locally grown. The study, which includes an English summary, reveals that while consumption patterns are determined by levels of income, both rich and poor households consumed imported rice; the former because they have internalized Western habits, the latter because of the ease of its preparation within a modern urban setting and work-styles.

203 **Le foncier et l'urbain – le cas d'une ville moyenne sahélienne:**
**Ouahigouya.** (Land tenure and the urban denominator, the case of a
medium-sized Sahelian town, Ouahigouya.)
B. Ganne. In: *Espaces disputés en Afrique noire*, edited by
B. Crousse (et al.). Paris: Karthala, 1986, p. 145-62.

An examination of land conflicts within a middle-sized town in northern Burkina Faso,
illustrating how recourse to traditional land tenure law favours speculation, while the
invocation of modern land tenure law and the judicial system conceals a simple conflict
between old and new forces battling for control of land. An English summary is
supplied.

204 **Political conflict and revolution in an African town.**
Elliott Percival Skinner. *American Anthropologist*, vol. 74, (Oct.
1973), p. 1205-17.

This is an analysis of the process of change as urban and rural populations adapt to
modern life. In Ouagadougou a variety of social and political cliques emerged at
independence to 'claim rights to power and legitimacy' (p. 1208), resulting in much
more open conflict and competition, arguing powerfully that the 'inherent stability'
many had claimed for colonial peoples was really 'a function of exogenous political
factors', and that in reality conflict, strife and revolution might better be predicted
(p. 1208).

205 **Politique urbaine: une révolution au service de l'état.** (Urban policy: a
revolution in the service of the State.)
Alain Marie. *Politique Africaine* (Paris), no. 33 (1989), p. 27-38.

The CNR urban policy in Ouagadougou has two prime thrusts: allocation of peripheral
quarters and the renovation of the city centre. Stripped of ideology, Sankara's urban
policy of reorganizing old urban territorial boundaries reveals itself as primarily aiming
at constructing a strong centralized state and breaking down potential sources of
resistance. There is an English summary of the article.

206 **La réussite des petits entrepreneurs dans le secteur informel de**
**Ouagadougou.** (The success of small entrepreneurs in the informal
sector of Ouagadougou.)
Meine Pieter Van Dijk. *Tiers Monde* (Paris), vol. 21, no. 82 (1980),
p. 373-86. bibliog.

This survey of the informal sector in Ouagadougou in 1977 included 183,000 people
(73.2 per cent) of the total active population of 250,000. There are statistics about their
age, access to credit, prior experience, specific occupations, and the problems they face
in making a living.

207 **Le 'secteur informel' à Fada N'Gourma.** (The informal sector in Fada
N'Gourma.)
P. Sirven.   In: *Pauvreté et développement dans les pays tropicaux:
hommage à Guy Laserre.*   Bordeaux, France: University of Bordeaux
Institut de Géographie, 1989, p. 541-62.
An attempt to determine the importance of the informal sector in Fada N'Gourma, the
regional capital of the Gurma. The town's districts are dissected and the various
activities of the informal sector are examined, and the chapter concludes with an
overview of the impact of the informal sector on employment of young people. There
is a summary in English.

208 **Transitional urbanization in Upper Volta: the case of Ouagadougou, a
savannah capital.**
Gary Bricker, Soumana Traore.   In: *Development of urban systems in
Africa*, edited by B. A. Obudho, S. El-Shakh.   New York: Praeger,
1979, p. 177-95.
A study of Ouagadougou's urban renewal options. The city, with a minimal annual
squatter growth of ten per cent, is likely to become a vast slum by the mid-1990s. In
the absence of adequate finances for wide-scale municipal services the authors maintain
the UN Habitat project in the city's southern outskirts offers the only viable option: a
mix of self-upgrading of urban dwellers and subsidized extension of services.

**L'avortement et la loi.** (Abortion and the law.)
*See* item no. 249.

# Health and Medicine

209 **Acute respiratory infections: a longitudinal study of 151 children in Burkina Faso.**
T. Lang (et al.). *International Journal of Epidemiology* (Oxford), vol. 15, no. 4 (1986), p. 553-60.

A report on longitudinal research on children below the age of five in a rural village. Forty-four per cent of them were found to be ill, and 59 per cent of those had acute respiratory infection during the rainy season. Figures during the dry season were 48 per cent and 73 per cent respectively. The main risk factors for acute respiratory illness were diagnosed as malnutrition and high birth ranking.

210 **Causes de l'infécondité dans la Volta noire.** (Causes of infertility in the Black Volta.)
Anne Retel-Laurentin. Paris: Presses Universitaires de France, 1979. 100p.

Well known for her work on the Central African Republic, the author outlines the demography of the Bobo people, and the epidemiological and gynaecological problems afflicting them that result in very high levels of female infertility.

211 **Child survival in sub-Saharan Africa: structural means and individual capacity, a case study from Burkina Faso.**
Odile Frank, Mathias Dakuyo. New York: Population Council, 1985. 76p. bibliog.

A study of health, hygiene, child diseases and child mortality, with some suggestions of simple preventive means that can be adopted. Burkina Faso has one of the highest, if not the highest, percentage of child mortality in the world.

212 **The cost of health for all: a feasibility study from Upper Volta.**
Alfred Merkle. Eschborn, Germany: German Agency for Technical
Cooperation, 1982. 101p. bibliog.

Originally the author's University of London 1981 Master's thesis, the study assesses
problems and costs of health planning and universal medical care in Burkina Faso. For
a similar effort to determine the economic aspects of health delivery in a narrower area
see N. Prescott, 'The economics of blindness prevention in Upper Volta', *Social
Science and Medicine* (Oxford), vol. 19, no. 10 (1984), p. 1051-5.

213 **Coût énergetique comparé du puisage traditionnel de l'eau, du pompage
manuel et à pied au Burkina.** (Relative energy consumption of drinking
water carried on foot, retrieved by pumps or collected from natural
rainfall.)
T. A. Brun. In: *Les malnutritions dans les pays du tiers-monde*, edited
by D. Lemonnier, Y. Ingenbleck. Paris: INSERM, 1986, p. 285-92.

With the collection of drinking water for family households an onerous activity on
which many hours are spent daily, the relative energy expended in three forms of water
collection are calculated. The study concludes that malnutrition is further aggravated in
the country due to the high cost of energy involved in the daily trek to wells and back.

214 **Food consumption and energy expenditure among Mossi peasants.**
A. Thierry (et al.). *Africa Environment* (Dakar), no. 14-16 (1980),
p. 425-48. bibliog.

A determination of energy-expenditure levels for adult men and women during
different seasons, on the basis of surveys of working hours and the measurement of
activity by indirect calorimetry.

215 **Health for socio-economic development in Burkina Faso.**
Abdoul Salam Kabore. *Transafrica Forum* (Washington, DC), vol. 3,
no. 3 (Summer 1986) p. 45-50.

An assessment of the country's medical problems, and the efforts mounted by the
revolutionary régime to resolve them, written by the Minister of Health. With life
expectancy at thirty-two years in rural areas, an overall infant mortality rate of 182 per
1,000 live births, one doctor per 44,000 people and one pharmacist per 85,160, the
situation remains precarious.

216 **Low utilization of community health workers: results from a household
interview survey in Burkina Faso.**
R. Sauerborn (et al.). *Social Science and Medicine* (Oxford), vol. 29,
no. 10 (1989), p. 1163-74.

Basing their research on a representative sample of households, the authors examine the
utilization of community health workers in comparison to other agents of health care. The
results are stark. In instances of both minor and serious illnesses, community health
workers are completely bypassed: in the first instance in favour of traditional healers, and
in the second to an even greater extent (96.5 per cent), in favour of professional health
agents. The policy implications of these results are explored in depth.

## Health and Medicine

217 **Norms and behaviour in Burkinabe fertility.**
James Trussell (et al.). *Population Studies* (London), vol. 43, no. 3 (1989), p. 489-54.

Using several methodologies, including survey analysis, the authors explore the low birth-levels in Bobo-Dioulasso, and the biological, medical and behavioural determinants of this.

218 **L'onchocercose, une endémie en voie de disparition au Burkina Faso.**
(River blindness, an endemic disease about to disappear in Burkina Faso.)
G. Neuvy. *Cahiers d'Outre-mer* (Bordeaux), no. 168 (1989), p. 377-93.

A discussion (which includes an English summary) of the final disappearance in 1988 of river blindness, hitherto one of Burkina Faso's most serious health problems. A considerable amount of literature exists on the various other diseases endemic in the country. See, for example, V. Robert (et al.), 'Malaria transmission in three sites surrounding Bobo-Dioulasso, Burkina Faso', *Bulletin of the Society of Vector Ecologists* (London), vol. 12, no. 2 (1987), p. 541-3, and A. Bosman (et al.), 'Further observations on chemoprophylaxis and prevalence of malaria using questionnaire data in urban and rural areas of Burkina Faso', *Parasitologia* (London), vol. 30, no. 2-3 (1988), p. 257-62.

219 **Paysages et milieux épidémiologiques dans l'espace ivoiro-burkinabe.**
(Epidemiological environments in the Ivory Coast–Burkina region.)
Gerard Remy. Paris: CNRS, 1988. 267p. maps. bibliog.

A thorough outline of the environmental variables that facilitate the appearance and diffusion of a host of contagious diseases in the Ivory Coast and Burkina Faso. There are several useful maps pinpointing spatial risk-areas, frequency and intensity of epidemics, and the study concludes with a detailed medical bibliography organized by disease categories.

220 **La santé publique en Haute-Volta: profil sanitaire.** (Public health in Upper Volta: a sanitary profile.)
F. Martin-Samos. Ouagadougou: CVRS, 1976. 202p.

A sanitary profile of Burkina Faso, full of data on clinics, health services, midwives, manpower, school health services, levels of disease by category of population, health budget and foreign aid for medical purposes. Despite serious advances, Burkina Faso still has one of the worst health profiles in Africa, as well as one of the lowest ratios of doctors to patients in the world. For an account of attempts to develop adequate mental health facilities, see G. Mitelberg (et al.), 'Projet de développement de la santé mentale au Burkina Faso' (A project to develop mental health in Burkina Faso), *Psychopathologie Africaine* (Paris), vol. 21, no. 1 (1986/7), p. 19-65.

# Youth and Education

221 **Le cas du Burkina Faso.** (The case of Burkina Faso.)
In: *Le syndrome du diplôme et le chômage des jeunes diplômés en Afrique francophone au sud du Sahara.* Addis Ababa: Organisation Internationale du Travail, Programme des Emplois et des Compétences Techniques pour l'Afrique, 1985, vol. 5, [n.p.]. bibliog.
A survey of schooling and employment prospects for high-school graduates. The author concludes that both are bleak in Burkina Faso.

222 **The Dinderosso Forestry School: case study of extension forestry training in Burkina Faso.**
Robert T. Winterbottom, Peter E. Linehan. *Rural Africana* (East Lansing, Michigan), no. 23/24 (1985/86), p. 107-14.
A survey of a vocational training programme.

223 **Education finance simulation model.**
Manuel Zymelman, Fonald K. Yee. Washington, DC: The World Bank, 1984. 59p.
This report to the World Bank stresses the fact that dramatic growth in school attendance rates is possible in Burkina Faso under several conditions tested by mathematical models. The most effective one is through the 'creation of a new type of teacher who would command a lower salary' (p. 17).

224 **Etude sur la délinquance juvenile en Haute-Volta.** (A study on juvenile delinquency in Upper Volta.)
Ouagadougou: Société Africaine d'Etudes et de Développement, 1977. 51p.
Overview of the prevalence of juvenile delinquency, and the procedures adopted to alleviate it. For a more comprehensive but somewhat dated study, see Jean Hochette,

## Youth and Education

*Inadaptation sociale et délinquance juvénile en Haute-Volta* (Paris: CNRS, 1968. 204p. bibliog.).

225 **L'innovation en Haute-Volta: éducation rurale et enseignement primaire.** (Innovation in Upper Volta: rural education and primary instruction.) Raymond Lallez. Paris: Les Presses de l'UNESCO, 1976. 107p. bibliog.

A survey of the innovative centres of rural education in Upper Volta, some of their recurrent problems and subsequent structural and educational changes. The work includes detailed study plans.

226 **Les jeunes ruraux en dehors de l'école.** (Young rural children outside school.) J. Christol. *Carnets Enfance* (Paris), vol. 8 (June 1968), p. 149-60.

Christol states that the inadequate educational system in rural areas was not coping with new school intakes and that many children were bypassed by the educational system altogether. Experimental youth programmes, such as Service Civique, and other attempts at rural animation and encouraging sporting activities were mounted but both the demographic and economic limitations of the country severely restrict the extent of these activities.

227 **Scoutisme rural: implantation, expansion, développement, vie et pédagogie du scoutisme dans les zones rurales en Haute-Volta.** (Scouting in rural areas: implantation, expansion, development, life and pedagogy of the Scout mouvement in the rural areas of Upper Volta.) Melegue Traore. Geneva: Bureau Mondial du Scoutisme, 1982. 149p.

A study of the Scout movement in rural areas of Burkina Faso.

228 **Upper Volta.** Martena Sasnett, Inez Sepmeyer. In: *Educational systems of Africa.* Berkeley, California: University of California Press, 1967, p. 738-46.

An outline of the country's educational system, from primary school to tertiary education; the different degrees, licences and diplomas offered; and the subject-teaching programmes and the number of hours allocated to each. See also the rather dated *Situations et perspectives de l'enseignement en Haute-Volta* (Situations and perspectives of teaching in Upper Volta) (Paris: UNESCO, 1961. 153p.); and 'L'adaptation de l'enseignement aux réalités Africaines en Haute-Volta' (The adaptation of teaching to the African reality in Upper Volta), *Nations Nouvelles* (Paris), (March 1966), p. 27-39, which discusses the unique problems of education in Burkina Faso at each level, with special reference to rural, adult and technical education.

# Politics

229 **Africa's new hope for democracy.**
Richard Vengroff. *Africa Report* (New York), (July-Aug. 1978),
p. 59-64.

Detailed report on the political parties and their platforms that ushered in Burkina
Faso's 1978 Third Republic under General Lamizana. For a more comprehensive study
see Hermann Yaméogo, *La IIIe République voltaïque* (The Third Voltaic Republic)
(Koudougou, Burkina Faso: Imprimerie des Quatre-Vents, 1990. 253p.). For a critical
assessment of the Third Republic, see Richard Vengroff, 'Soldiers and civilians in the
Third Republic', *Africa Report* (New York), (Jan.-Feb. 1980), p. 4-8.

230 **Les années Sankara: de la révolution à la rectification.** (The Sankara
years: from the revolution to the rectification.)
Bruno Jaffre. Paris: Harmattan, 1989. 332p.

Jaffre's comprehensive study of the Sankara era reviews all aspects of domestic policy –
cultural, economic, social – and foreign policy initiatives and reforms. He also devotes
considerable attention to the causes of the putsch of 15 October 1987 which saw
Sankara's death at the hands of his former friend, Blaise Campaore. An annex of
political chronology, acronyms and extracts from various discourses completes the
book. For an equally valuable account of the Sankara era, see Pierre Englebert, *La
révolution burkinabe* (The Burkinabe revolution) (Paris, Harmattan, 1987. 270p.)
which includes an annex of documents and key pronouncements by Sankara. The
Popular Front which replaced Sankara published its own assessment of four years of
revolutionary action in *Assises nationales sur le bilan des 4 années de révolution*
(Ouagadougou: Front Populaire, 1988. 150p.).

231 **Blaise Campaore. The architect of Burkina Faso's revolution.**
Ben Obinwa Ninji. Ibadan, Nigeria: Spectrum Books, 1989. 88p.

A blustering effort by a Nigerian journalist who originally supported Sankara's rise to
power, to legitimate Campaore's credentials as the true Burkinabe revolutionary. The
author argues that Sankara rapidly strayed from the ideals of the revolution, making

**Politics**

Campaore's coup d'état ('rectification process') inevitable. See also Joan Baxter, Keith Somerville, 'Burkina Faso' in *Benin, the Congo and Burkina Faso: economics, politics, society*, edited by Chris Allen (et al.) (London: Pinter, 1989, p. 247-86, bibliog.). In due course Campaore was forced to hold competitive elections, the run-up to which is discussed in Russell Geekie, 'Campaore's campaign', *Africa Report* (New York), vol. 36, no. 5 (Sept.-Oct. 1991), p. 55-8.

232 **Burkina Faso: a revolution derailed.**
Ernest Harsch. *Africa Report* (New York), (Jan.-Feb. 1988), p. 33-9.
A discussion of the 1987 coup, a 'derailment of the relationship of trust and confidence between the people and the government' (p. 39). Despite whatever mistakes Sankara might have made, visible popular anger at his death and continued suspicion of Campaore's successor régime, underline the degree to which Sankara's leadership had struck roots in society. For an assessment of Campaore's 'far from secure' support in the country, and some of his reforms, see Ernest Harsch, 'How popular is the Front', *Africa Report* (New York), vol. 34, no. 1 (Jan.-Feb. 1989), p. 56-61.

233 **Burkina Faso: between feeble state and total state, the swing continues.**
René Otayek.  In: *Contemporary West African states*, edited by Donal B. Cruise O'Brien (et al.).  Cambridge, England: Cambridge University Press, 1989, p. 13-30.
A compact summary of the political experience of Burkina Faso since independence, the revolutionary matrix imposed by the charismatic Thomas Sankara, and the reasons for his demise in 1987. The author concludes that 'by dint of wanting to re-organise everything, the CNR finished by destablising the society against which it had constructed itself' (p. 23). All of its policies, laudable though they might have been, were impractical, or triggered unintended results, since the organization 'did not have the means to realise the changes it desired. Without a real grip on society it found itself alone and confronted with itself' (p. 24). See also the author's 'Burkina Faso enters a new political phase: the sequel to the coup of 15 October 1987', *Journal of Communist Studies* (London), vol. 4, no. 2 (1988), p. 213-17. For the changed priorities of the successor Campaore régime, see René Otayek, 'Après le coup d'état du 15 octobre 1987, retour à la case départ au Burkina Faso' (Return to the starting point in Burkina Faso after the coup d'état of 15 October 1987), *Année Africaine 1987/8* (Paris: Pedone, 1987, p. 239-68.

234 **Combat pour l'Afrique.** (Struggle for Africa.)
Daniel Ouezzin Coulibaly.  Abidjan: Les Nouvelles Editions Africaines, 1985. 531p.
Assembled by Claude Gérard, and with an introduction by the President of Côte d'Ivoire Houphouët-Boigny, this work is a collection of the speeches of Coulibaly (1909-58), one of Burkina Faso's and French West Africa's early RDA (Rassemblement Démocratique Africain) political leaders, who in one capacity or another participated in all of the colonial structures set up by France between 1946 and 1958.

235   **The death of Thomas Sankara and the rectification of the people's revolution in Burkina Faso.**
Michael Wilkins.   *African Affairs* (London), vol. 88, no. 352 (1989), p. 375-88.

A critical assessment of the concrete aspects of Campaore's 'rectification' of Sankara's deviations from the ideals of the Burkinabe revolution. The author concludes that apart from token redistribution of uniforms in the armed forces, little has changed in Burkina Faso. Moreover, aware of the tenuousness of his own grip on power, Campaore has tried to ensure that 'no section of the Burkinabe nation are left out', the result being a retreat from both Sankara's revolutionary zeal and the latter's stress on economic nationalism. See also René Otayek's recent article 'The democratic "rectification" in Burkina Faso', *Journal of Communist Studies* (London), vol. 8, no. 2 (July 1992), p. 82-104.

236   **Du langage animalier en politique.** (On the use of animal language in politics.)
P. H. Euphorion.   *Genève-Afrique* (Geneva), vol. 26, no. 2 (1988), p. 97-105.

A brief but fascinating outline of how pejorative references to the animal world have become engrained in political discourse and propaganda in Burkina Faso. On the rôle and nature of propaganda see Claude Dubuch, 'Langage du pouvoir, pouvoir du langage' (The language of power, the power of language), *Politique Africaine* (Paris), no. 20 (1985), p. 44-53. For a critical view of the popular songs of praise for the Burkinabe revolution, see Edmond Jouve, 'Le Burkina Faso et ses chantiers de l'avenir' (Burkina Faso and its songs of the future), *Mondes et Cultures* (Paris), vol. 156, no. 3 (1986), p. 607-15.

237   **Etat et société au Burkina Faso: essai sur la politique africaine.** (State and society in Burkina Faso: essay on African politics.)
Claudette Savonnet-Guyot.   Paris: Karthala, 1986. 227p. bibliog.

A comprehensive outline of traditional life and the political evolution of Burkina Faso, emphasizing the perennial tug-of-war between imported Western socio-economic and political concepts and pre-existing traditional African structures, and the manner in which these were moulded together by Sankara in his 1983 coup d'état. For a detailed chronology of the events leading to Sankara's seizure of power in 1983, written by a University of Ouagadougou Law School lecturer, see Larba Yarga, 'Les prémices a l'avènement du Conseil National de la Révolution en Haute Volta' (The beginnings of the National Council for the Revolution in Upper Volta), *Le Mois en Afrique* (Paris), no. 213/4 (Oct.-Nov. 1983), p. 24-41.

238   **Ideology and praxis in Thomas Sankara's populist revolution of 4 August 1983 in Burkina Faso.**
Guy Martin.   *Issue* (Los Angeles), Nno. 15 (1987), p. 77-90.

An enquiry into the origins and ideological roots of the 1983 revolution of Sankara. In another article the author sees in the revolution the implementation of Franz Fanon's ideas; see Guy Martin, 'Actualité de Fanon: convergences dans la pensée politique de Franz Fanon et de Thomas Sankara' (The presence of Fanon: parallels in the political ideas of Franz Fanon and Thomas Sankara), *Genève-Afrique* (Geneva), vol. 25, no. 2 (1987), p. 103-22. [An English summary is included.] For a Marxist interpretation (by

**Politics**

Sankara's Press director) of the dialectics leading to the 1983 revolution, see Babou Paulin Bamouni, *Burkina Faso. Processus de la révolution* (Burkina Faso: the revolutionary process) (Paris, Harmattan, 1986. 189p.). For other discussions of the same topic, see the brief articles grouped under 'Feature: Burkina Faso', *Journal of African Marxists* (London), no. 11 (Feb. 1989), p. 54-75. For a highly didactic discussion underpinned by Marxist philosophy, of the need for State planning, see Jacques Peyrega, *L'émergence de la notion et la réalisation de la planification socialiste* (The emergence of the notion and the realization of socialist planning) (Ouagadougou: University of Ouagadougou, 1985. 82p.). A critical assessment of 'Burkinabe socialism' is provided by an economist at the Central Bank of France, Bernard Cherlonneix, in his 'La voie burkinabe vers le socialisme?' (The Burkinabe road to socialism?), *Le Mois en Afrique* (Paris), no. 247/8 (1986), p. 4-14.

239 **Il s'appelait Sankara: chronique d'une mort violente.** (His name was Sankara: chronicle of a violent death.)
Sennen Andriamirado. Paris: Editions Jeune-Afrique, 1989. 187p.

A detailed review of events leading to the 1987 coup, the assassination of Burkina Faso's charismatic leader, Thomas Sankara, and the sequence of events in its aftermath. The Malagasy author Andriamirado, Head Editor of the influential weekly *Jeune-Afrique*, was personally familiar with Sankara, current President Blaise Campaore (who overthrew Sankara), and other key figures in Burkina Faso, and provides rich detail not available in other accounts. See also Valere D. Some, *Thomas Sankara: l'espoir assassiné* (Thomas Sankara: hope assassinated) (Paris, Harmattan, 1990. 230p.).

240 **The political orientation speech delivered by Captain Thomas Sankara in Ouagadougou on 2 October 1983.**
In: *Military Marxist regimes in Africa*, edited by John Markakis, Michael Waller. London: Frank Cass, 1986, p. 145-66.

The full text of the much-cited and seminal speech of Sankara in which he outlines the bitter heritage of 'twenty-three years of neo-colonialism' since independence, and the precise re-orientation needed to attain self-sufficiency and national dignity. Extracts from the speech are widely found in other sources, including *Review of African Political Economy* (London), no. 32 (April 1985), p. 48-55.

241 **Réorganisation économique et résistances sociales: la question des alliances au Burkina.** (Economic reorganization and social resistances: the question of alliances in Burkina Faso.)
Pascal Labazée. *Politique Africaine* (Paris), no. 20 (Dec. 1985), p. 10-28.

Sankara's 1983 revolution is considered from the perspective of the radically different social, political and economic alliances which resulted. The upheaval brought about a decline in the power of traditional Mossi chiefs and the rise of a central–rural alliance in an effort to attain self-sufficiency and self-reliance. For a deeper exploration of Sankara's ultimate disenfranchisement of traditional chiefs, see Claudette Savonnet-Guyot, 'Le Prince et le Naobe' (The Prince and the Naobe), *Politique Africaine* (Paris), no. 20 (Dec. 1985), p. 29-43. For modifications of some of Sankara's policies and alliances in the latter years of his reign see Pascal Labazée, 'Discours et contrôle politique: les avatars du sankarisme' (Speeches and political control: the avatars of

Sankarism), *Politique Africaine* (Paris), no. 33 (March 1989), p. 11-26. This last article includes an English summary.

242 **The revolutionary process in Burkina Faso: breaks and continuities.**
René Otayek. In: *Military Marxist regimes in Africa*, edited by John Markakis, Michael Waller. London: Frank Cass, 1986, p. 82-100.
An analysis of the nature of the revolutionary government that came to power in 1983 and why it differed so dramatically from other military régimes. According to Otayek, it 'represents in Weberian terms the ideal type of radical military regime. Few other regimes correspond so perfectly to this ideal type' (p. 98). The chapter is a reprint from an article that first appeared in *Journal of Communist Studies* (London), vol. 1, no. 3/4 (1986).

243 **Sankara and the Burkinabe revolution.**
Elliott Percival Skinner. *Journal of Modern African Studies*, vol. 26, no. 3 (Sept. 1988), p. 437-55.
Analysis of the attainments and constraints in Sankara's Burkina Faso by a former Columbia University anthropologist and US Ambassador (1966-69) to the country. Notwithstanding a multitude of laudable reforms he initiated, Sankara's 'personal impetuosity . . . sudden and improvised decisions . . . ultimately sapped the cohesion of the National Council of the Revolution' (p. 455) leading to his bloody assassination.

244 **Sankara, Campaore et la révolution burkinabe.** (Sankara, Campaore and the Burkinabe revolution.)
Ludo Martens, Milde Meesters. Antwerp, Belgium: Epo, 1989. 332p.
Based on extensive archival research and interviews, this is a study of the roots, evolution and political positions of the seven parties of the Left that emerged with the revolution of 1983, and an outline of Sankara's major policy innovations.

245 **Sankara le rebelle.** (Sankara, the rebel.)
Sennen Andriamirado. Paris: Editions Jeune-Afrique, 1987. 237p.
A laudatory overview of Thomas Sankara's rise to power, his formative years, personal characteristics, the roots of his charisma, and the nature of the policies he espoused that so electrified both Burkina Faso and much of Africa. See also Jean Ziegler, *Sankara, un nouveau pouvoir africain* (Sankara, a new African power) (Paris: Editions Pierre-Marcel Favre, 1986. 176p.).

246 **The struggle for stability in Upper Volta.**
Victor D. Du Bois. *American University Field Staff Reports* (Hanover, New Hampshire), vol. 12, no. 1-5 (1969). bibliog. (West Africa Series).
Five reports, of between eleven and fifteen pages each, tracing the colonial period, the early years of the Yaméogo presidency, the coup d'état that terminated it, and the early years of the General Lamizana administration.

## Politics

247 **Thomas Sankara speaks: the Burkina Faso revolution 1983-87.**
New York: Pathfinder, 1988. 260p.

A selection of Sankara's various speeches at home and abroad, the majority of which
had previously not been available in English. The work includes an introduction by
Doug Cooper, a general chronology for the years 1949-79, and a more detailed one for
1980-87. For a similar, though somewhat more comprehensive work see David
Gakunzi (ed.), *Thomas Sankara. 'Oser inventer l'avenir'. La parole de Sankara*
('Daring to invent the future'. The words of Sankara) (Paris: Harmattan, 1991. 290p.).

248 **Le tripartisme dans le droit public voltaïque.** (Tripartism in Voltaic
public law.)
Larba Yarga. *Le Mois en Afrique* (Paris), no. 174/5 (June-July 1980),
p. 114-29.

A survey of Burkina Faso's electoral and political history, with an emphasis on the
parties that emerged in each specific era. Written by a University of Ouagadougou law
instructor and former constitutional counsellor to the Supreme Court, the article is
very useful because of its data on the various political formations.

**Evolution de la Haute Volta de 1898 au 3 janvier 1966.** (Evolution of Upper
Volta from 1898 to 3 January 1966.)
*See* item no. 37.

**Syndicalisme et démocratie en Afrique noire: l'expérience du Burkina Faso
(1936-1988).** (Syndicalism and democracy in Black Africa; the experience of
Burkina Faso, 1936-88.)
*See* item no. 142.

# The Constitution and Legal System

249 **L'avortement et la loi.** (Abortion and the law.)
Frédéric Titinga Pacéré. Ouagadougou: Imprimerie Nouvelle du
Centre, 1983. 69p.
An outline of the incidence of abortion in Burkina Faso and of the public law and
legislation on abortion.

250 **Burkina Faso: une nouvelle forme de justice à l'essai.** (Burkina Faso: an
experiment in a new kind of justice.)
Pierre Meyer. *Afrique Contemporaine* (Paris), no. 156 (1990), p. 51-6.
Meyer reviews the post-1983 changes in the legal system and its structures in Burkina
Faso, including the creation of Popular Revolutionary Tribunals.

251 **Code des personnes et de la famille.** (Personal and family law.)
Ouagadougou: Imprimerie Nationale, 1989. 215p.
The statutes of personal law in Burkina Faso are reprinted in this work.

252 **Code de procédure pénale, suivi des décrets d'application.** (Criminal
procedure law, followed by rules of application.)
Ouagadougou: Imprimerie Nationale de la Haute-Volta, 1989. 328p.
The official handbook on criminal law and the specific procedures of its application in
Burkina Faso, prepared by the Ministry of Justice. The book includes a very useful
index.

## The Constitution and Legal System

253 **Community values, domestic tranquillity and customary law in Upper Volta.**
Carol Bohmer. *Journal of Modern African Studies* (Cambridge), vol. 16, no. 2 (June 1978), p. 295-310.

A study of how the rôle of customary law has declined in Burkina Faso. Focusing on the court of Bobo-Dioulasso (the country's second-largest town), which as a tribunal of the first instance handles family law and other disputes over sums up to $200, the author concludes that 'customary courts may not in fact apply customary law' (p. 295). The court keeps no records, does not refer to precedents, calls upon no experts on oral tradition, has no guide to the customary law of the various ethnic groups within its jurisdiction, and, even more significantly, shows little interest in the ethnic or religious background of plaintiffs, ruling in a 'modern' manner, within the general context of the country's cultural values.

254 **Connaissance de l'organisation politique, institutionnelle et administrative du Burkina Faso.** (Knowledge of the political, administrative and constitutional organization of Burkina Faso.)
Jacques Bougma. Ouagadougou: J. Bougma, 1988. 75p.

An outline of Burkina Faso's political, constitutional, administrative and legal organization, as defined in the Constitution and other statutes. Several annexes include seminal decrees of the Sankara régime. The volume was prepared for study and examination purposes of the country's administrative cadres.

255 **Constitution du Burkina Faso.** (The constitution of Burkina Faso.)
Ouagadougou: Editions Sidwaya, 1991. 51p.

The text of the Constitution adopted and promulgated in June 1991.

256 **La constitution voltaïque du 27 novembre 1977.** (The Voltaic constitution of 27 November 1977.)
Patrick Cadenat. *Revue Juridique et Politique* (Paris), vol. 32, no. 4 (Oct.-Dec. 1978), p. 1025-36.

An analysis of the text of the constitutional provisions of 1977 which bear similarities to those of the French Fifth Republic, with a considerably strengthened Presidency. See also Joseph Owona, 'La constitution de la IIIe République voltaïque' (The constitution of the Third Voltaic Republic), *Penant* (Paris), vol. 89, no. 765 (July-Sept. 1979), p. 309-28. For the text itself see 'Texte de la constitution voltaïque' (Text of the Voltaic constitution), *Afrique Contemporaine* (Paris), no. 95 (Jan.-Feb. 1978), p. 23-31. For the country's first post-independence structures and provisions see Joseph Conombo, 'Les institutions et leur développement en République de Haute-Volta' (The institutions and their development in the republic of Upper Volta), in *The constitutions and administrative institutions of the new states* (Brussels: Institut International des Civilisations Différents, 1965, p. 98-102). For the emergency powers lodged in the Presidency in Burkina Faso's 1959-80 constitutions, traceable to influences from provisions in the Fifth French Republic, see Larba Yarga, 'Les pouvoirs exceptionnels du Président de la République dans les constitutions voltaïques de 1959 a 1980' (The extraordinary presidential powers in the Voltaic constitutions from 1958 to 1980), *Revue Juridique et Politique* (Paris), vol. 34, no. 3 (July-Sept. 1980), p. 730-8.

The Constitution and Legal System

257  **Le développement du droit judiciaire au Burkina Faso.** (The
development of judicial law in Burkina Faso.)
Jacques Delouvroy. *Revue Juridique et Politique* (Paris), vol. 91, no. 3
(1987), p. 228-44.
An examination of Burkina Faso's legal system, and especially the judicial reforms
since the 1983 revolution. The author sees major advances as well as dangers in some
of the reforms which include greater weight to local custom. For a survey of legal
institutions and the judiciary in the 1960s see P. Marchand, 'L'organisation judiciaire
en Haute-Volta' (The judicial system in Upper Volta), *Penant* (Paris) (Jan.-March
1964), p. 121-9.

258  **Droit financier et bancaire.** (Financial and banking law.)
A. Daloze.  Ouagadougou: Université de Ouagadougou, 1989. 102p.
Commercial law, banking law and credit regulations of Burkina Faso.

259  **Le droit privé des Mossi: tradition et évolution.** (Mossi private law:
tradition and evolution.)
Robert Pageard.  Paris: CNRS, 1969. 2 vols. bibliog.
Based on Pageard's first-hand experience as a judge in Ouagadougou between 1960
and 1964, this work outlines in detail the basic tenets of the Mossi social order, and the
rôle of the individual and inter-personal relationships within it. The author then
proceeds to detail the rights, duties and obligations that stem from this world-outlook,
as reflected in traditional Mossi customary law relating to, amongst other things,
marriage and divorce, chiefs and youth. See also Diallo Seyni Sambo, 'Les droits de
famille dans la coutume Mossi' (Customary family law among the Mossi), *Penant*
(Paris), no. 715 (Jan.-March 1967), p. 13-31 and no. 716 (April-June 1967), p. 151-65.

260  **Les droits des étrangers au Burkina Faso.** (The rights of foreigners in
Burkina Faso.)
Deen Gibrila.  *Penant* (Paris), vol. 95, no. 786/7 (Jan.-June 1985),
p. 37-52.
Gibrila, Director of Studies at the National School of Administration in Ouagadougou,
outlines the status of foreigners under Burkinabe private and public law.

261  **Les enfants abandonnés: faits, droits et protection.** (Abandoned
children: facts, laws and protection.)
Frédéric Titinga Pacéré.  Ouagadougou: F. T. Pacéré. 1989, 85p.
A survey of the rules and laws relating to abandoned children in Burkina Faso, written
and distributed by a prolific Burkinabe lawyer.

262  **Journal Officiel du Burkina Faso.** (Official Journal of Burkina Faso.)
Ouagadougou: Imprimerie Nationale. 1983-  . weekly.
A journal which publishes the parliamentary record of the official acts of Burkina
Faso. Before the country's name-change the publication was called *Journal Officiel de
la République de Haute-Volta*; and during the colonial era, *Journal Officiel de la Haute-
Volta*. Between 1948 and 1953 Upper Volta was merged with Ivory Coast; for acts for
this period see the *Journal Officiel de la Côte-d'Ivoire*, published in Abidjan.

## The Constitution and Legal System

263 **La justice populaire au Burkina Faso.** (Popular justice in Burkina
Faso.)
Ouagadougou: Ministère de la Justice, 1986. 99p.
An official publication on the administration of justice and the court system of Burkina
Faso.

264 **Le mariage en Haute Volta: option entre monogamie et polygamie.**
(Marriage in Upper Volta: option between monogamy and polygamy.)
Mamadou Sawadogo. *Penant* (Paris), vol. 95, no. 786/7 (Jan.-June
1985), p. 53-7.
An account of marriage law in Burkina Faso, written by a leading Burkinabe lawyer
based in Paris. For the country's revised family code, see also F. M. Sawadogo, 'Le
nouveau code burkinabe de la famille: principes essentiels et perspectives d'application'
(The new Burkinabe family law: essential principles and guidelines for application),
*Revue Juridique et Politique* (Paris), vol. 44, no. 3 (1990), p. 372-406. See also Hilde
Nuytinck, 'Les principes du nouveau droit de la famille au Burkina Faso' (The
principles of the new family law in Burkina Faso), *Penant* (Paris), no. 806 (June-Oct.
1991), p. 258-75.

265 **Le nouveau code d'investissements au Burkina: changement ou
continuité.** (The new investment code in Burkina Faso: change and
continuity.)
Filiga Michel Sawadogo. *Revue Juridique et Politique* (Paris), vol. 90,
no. 1/2 (1986), p. 63-93.
Sawadogo outlines the new investment law of 7 August 1984, aimed at attracting
foreign investments while protecting Burkina Faso from exploitation. For additional
material, see Filiga Michel Sawadogo and Pierre Meyer, 'Droit, état et société: le cas
du Burkina Faso' (Law, state and society: the case of Burkina Faso), *Revue de Droit
International et Droit Comparé* (Paris), vol. 64, no. 3 (1987), p. 225-42.

266 **L'organisation judiciaire au Burkina Faso et le destin de la Chambre
Constitutionnel.** (The judicial organization of Burkina Faso and the
destiny of the Constitutional Chamber.)
Aimé Nikiéma, Salif Yonaba. *Penant* (Paris), no. 791 (July-Oct.
1986), p. 287-301.
An outline of Burkina's judicial system headed by its Constitutional Court.

267 **Le participation des travailleurs dans les entreprises publiques
burkinabe.** (Worker participation in the Burkinabe state enterprises.)
Filiga Michel Sawadogo. *Penant* (Paris), vol. 95 no..788/9 (July-Dec.
1985), p. 199-218.
Statutory law relating to workers' participation in the management of Burkina Faso's
parastatals, summarized by the Director of Studies at the School of Law of the
University of Ouagadougou. For the legal rights of workers, see S. Sawadogo,
'L'entreprise et les droits de l'homme: les protections instituées au Burkina'
(Businesses and human rights: protections established in Burkina Faso), *Revue
Juridique et Politique* (Paris), vol. 43, no. 3/4 (1989), p. 361-70. See also Filiga Michel

Sawadogo, P. Kienda, 'La réforme du droit des entreprises publiques voltaïques par les ordonnances du 1 juin 1982' (The reform of the code of Voltaic public enterprises in the ordinances of 1 June 1983), *Revue Voltaïque du Droit* (Ouagadougou), no. 4 (June 1983), p. 119-48.

268 **Recueil annoté des textes applicables au droit du travail au Burkina Faso.** (Annotated collection of texts on labour law in Burkina Faso.)
R. Coppieters't Wallant, Karim Ouattara. Ouagadougou: Chambre de Commerce, d'Industrie et d'Artisanat, 1990. 2nd ed. 465p. bibliog.
Comprehensive compilation of Burkina Faso's labour law and legislation relating to labour.

269 **Régime financier de l'Etat et des collectivités locales.** (Finance law of the State and of local communities.)
Ouagadougou: Ministère des Finances, 1988. 7th ed. 135p.
The public finance law of Burkina Faso is discussed in this official publication.

270 **Réglementation des marchés administratifs.** (Regulations on public contracts.)
Ouagadougou: Chambre de Commerce, d'Industrie et d'Artisanat, 1989. 169p.
Assembled and published by the Burkina Faso Chamber of Commerce, this work is the standard compilation of law and legislation relating to Burkinabe public contracts.

271 **La République de Haute-Volta.** (The Republic of Upper Volta.)
Philippe Lippens. Paris: Berger-Levrault, 1972. 62p. bibliog.
Published for the International Institute of Public Administration (Paris), the work includes the text and a discussion of the Voltaic constitution of 29 June 1970, an outline of the country's society and salient aspects of its political evolution to 1972. This volume forms part of the Political and Constitutional Encyclopedia of Africa series (P. F. Gonidec).

272 **La structure dualiste du droit au Burkina Faso.** (The dualist structure of law in Burkina Faso.)
M. P. Meyer. *Penant* (Paris), no. 790-1 (Jan.-July 1986), p. 77-89.
A discussion of the legal problems posed by the parallel existence in Burkina Faso of written (positive) and customary (oral) law.

273 **Le traitement fiscale inégalitaire des entreprises au Burkina Faso: le cas de l'imposition des bénéfices.** (Unequal fiscal treatment of Burkina Faso enterprises: the case of taxation of profits.)
Filiga Michel Sawadogo. *Le Mois en Afrique* (Paris), vol. 21, no. 239/ 40 (Jan. 1986), p. 54-68.
After a comprehensive examination of fiscal and taxation policy in Sankara's Burkina Faso, the author argues against the unequal taxation of enterprises, private and public.

# The Constitution and Legal System

Lowering of taxes would encourage the entry of new risk capital that is both sorely needed and also worth any additional administrative expenditures that might ensue.

274 **Les tribunaux populaires de la révolution en Haute Volta.** (The popular tribunals of the revolution in Upper Volta.) Michel F. Sawadogo, Larba Yarga. *Penant* (Paris), vol. 94, no. 785 (July-Sept. 1984), p. 267-83.

The legal statutes, mandate and composition of the revolutionary tribunals set up in Burkina Faso under Sankara to deal with white-collar crime. See also Ignace Yerbanga, Martin Zonou, 'L'administration de la preuve devant les tribunaux populaires de la révolution au Burkina' (The presentation of proof before the popular tribunals of the revolution in Burkina), *Revue Juridique et Politique* (Paris), vol. 39 no. 1/2 (Jan.-March 1985), p. 62-8.

275 **Upper Volta.**
In: *Water law in selected African countries*, edited by Dante A. Caponera. Rome: Food and Agricultural Organization, 1979, p. 224-42.

A survey of water law in Upper Volta as of the late 1970s, together with a listing of all relevant legislation in force at that time.

# Administration

276 **Administration et développement au Burkina Faso.** (Administration and development in Burkina Faso.)
Toulouse, France: Presses de l'Institut d'Etudes Politiques de Toulouse, 1987. 324p. bibliog.
A joint effort by Burkinabe and French scholars to focus on the relationship between public administration and development. The work includes twelve contributions on topics such as the country's investment code, local administration, administrative justice, sub-ministerial coordination, and the civil service.

277 **Contribution à l'étude des styles de management en Afrique: le cas de Burkina Faso.** (Contribution to the study of styles of management in Africa: the example of Burkina Faso.)
Boukary Savadogo. Ouagadougou: Université de Ouagadougou, Centre d'Etudes, de Documentation et de Recherches Economiques et Sociales, 1986. 183p. bibliog.
A comprehensive overview of public administration theory and style, and its applicability to Burkina Faso. The study ends with a list of thirty-six public companies and information including their acronyms, details of their staff, business turnover, date of creation, and capitalization.

278 **Deux cas d'ouvrages clé en main au Burkina.** (Two cases of leased enterprises in Burkina.)
Emile Toe Badou, Franck Sibila Campaore. *Revue Juridique et Politique* (Paris), vol. 42, no. 2-3 (1988), p. 185-96.
Based on concrete experience of two contracted-out enterprises, the authors – the president of the Bobo-Dioulasso court of appeals and the district attorney at the same court – argue against any such future arrangements except with verifiably viable entities.

## Administration

279 **La fonction du personnel au Burkina Faso.** (Personnel management in Burkina Faso.)
Jean Claude Quéré. Ouagadougou: Université de Ouagadougou, Centre d'Etudes, de Documentation et de Recherches Economiques et Sociales, 1986. 177p.

Quéré discusses personnel management theory, and follows this with an analysis of the Burkinabe ideological, cultural, structural and economic context, and the resultant problems.

280 **Révolution voltaïque et réforme de l'administration territoriale.** (Voltaic revolution and the reform of the territorial administration.)
Jean de Bois Gaudusson. In: *Année Africaine 1983*. Paris: Pedone, 1983, p. 112-15, 127-44.

The new administrative structures set up subsequent to the 1983 revolution, including the full text of the ordinance.

# Foreign Policy and International Relations

**281  The bases of Ghana–Upper Volta relations during the Nkrumah regime.**
E. O. Saffu. *Canadian Journal of African Studies* (Ottawa), vol. 4, no. 2 (Spring 1970), p. 195-206.
A survey of Ghana–Upper Volta relations during the period 1957-66. Several factors played a differential rôle in determining the foreign policy of each country; domestic factors in general played a far more important rôle in Upper Volta, while ideology was the dominant determinant in Ghana.

**282  Burkina Faso: August 1983 – the beginning of delinking?**
Talata Kafando.  In: *Adjustment or delinking?* edited by Azzam Mahjoob.  London: Zed Press, 1990, p. 109-30.
A discussion of Burkina Faso's acute economic dependency and the resultant pre-Sankara neo-colonial development policies. Cooperation with the Arab countries (South–South links) also brought 'very meagre' results, being basically 'an extension of North–South cooperation'. To break with the 'mechanisms of imperialist domination' (p. 121) requires an original policy of development such as that put forward by President Sankara in his 'political orientation' speech. For more on Burkina Faso–Arab economic relations see Talata Kafando, 'Coopération arabo-burkinabe: bilan et perspectives' (Arab–Burkinabe cooperation: assessment and prospects), *Africa Development* (Dakar), vol. 11, no. 2/3 (1986), p. 191-212. This last article has an English summary.

**283  The case concerning the frontier dispute Burkina Faso/Republic of Mali:**
*uti possidetis* **in an African context.**
G. J. Naldi.  *International and Comparative Law Quarterly* (London), vol. 36, part 4 (1987), p. 893-903.
An analysis of the origins of the Mali–Burkina Faso boundary dispute which on several occasions brought the two countries into military conflict, and was finally resolved by the International Court of Justice. See also Gilbert Some, 'Un exemple de conflit

79

## Foreign Policy and International Relations

frontalier: le différend entre la Haute-Volta et la Mali' (An example of a boundary dispute: the disagreement between Burkina and Mali), in *Année Africaine 1978* (Paris: Pedone, 1978, p. 339-70); Jean-Pierre Queneudec, 'Le règlement du différend frontalier Burkina Faso/Mali par la Cour Internationale de Justice' (The settlement of the boundary dispute between Burkina Faso and Mali by the International Court of Justice), *Revue Juridique et Politique* (Paris), vol. 42, no. 1 (1988), p. 29-41; and Howard French, 'Burkina Faso at the eye of a West African storm', *Africa Report* (New York) (Jan.-Feb. 1986), p. 28-30. The latter argues the rise to power of the militant Sankara embroiled Burkina Faso 'in nearly all of the region's intra-francophone squabbles' (p. 28) and that the border dispute with Mali was exacerbated by Sankara's crackdown on corruption in the regional CEAO (Communauté Economique d'Afrique Occidentale) organization and his arrest of its Malian Secretary General and other high officials for embezzlement.

284 **L'insertion régionale du régime Sankara entre pragmatisme et idéologie.** (The regional entry of the Sankara régime: between pragmatism and ideology.)
Leon C. Codo.    In: *Année Africaine 1984.* Paris: Pedone, 1986, p. 176-95.

Tracing international relations during the first year of Sankara régime, Codo underlines how the government's early hostility towards some of the country's neighbours (and especially the Ivory Coast) gave way to realism and pragmatism. A country-by-country summary of relations with Burkina Faso is included. For a further account of the early period which saw the rupture of diplomatic relations with the Ivory Coast, see Yves-André Faure, 'Ouaga et Abidjan: divorce à l'africaine?' (Ouaga and Abidjan: an African divorce?), *Politique Africaine* (Paris), no. 20 (Dec. 1985), p. 78-86.

285 **La politique extérieure de la Haute-Volta.** (The foreign policy of Upper Volta.)
Alain Faujas.    *Revue Française d'Etudes Politiques Africaines* (Paris), (Nov. 1972), p. 59-73.

Faujas describes the moderate, 'realistic' pro-Western foreign policy of Burkina Faso during its first decade of independence.

# The Economy, Trade and Commerce

286  **Aid implementation and administrative capacity in Upper Volta: a suggested methodology of assessment.**
Margaret Wolfson.  Paris: OECD, 1981. 30p. bibliog.
The author seeks to establish the country's capacity to absorb foreign aid that it so desperately needs, and to meet fiscal obligations arising from the recurrent costs of development programmes. The author's assessment is wholly negative, resting on the country's paucity of State revenues, the absence of a coherent development plan pinpointing priorities, and the lack of fiscal accountability of government structures.

287  **L'artisanat et les activités à Ouagadougou, Haute-Volta.** (Crafts and activities in Ouagadougou.)
G. Pallier.  Ouagadougou: Secrétariat d'Etat des Affaires Etrangères, 1970. 363p. bibliog.
A misleading title since the work surveys all aspects of economic activity in the Upper Volta of 1970. Among the major enterprises surveyed are water-storage facilities, electric companies and mines, followed by an encyclopaedic multi-faceted analysis (by ethnic group, region, sex, age and education) of all trade and small-scale artisan activity in the country, from the manufacture of building bricks and leather works, to the carving of masks for tourists. For a much briefer but more recent survey, see *Eleménts caractéristiques des entreprises du Burkina Faso* (Typical elements of Burkina Faso business enterprises) (Ouagadougou: Institut National de la Statistique, 1987. 31p.). The latter includes data on capitalization and business turnover.

288  **Burkina Faso.**
Anthon Slanagen.  In: *Rural finance profiles in African countries*, edited by Mario Masini.  Milan: Finafrica, 1989, vol. 2, p. 1-61.
A brief introduction to Burkina Faso's economy, followed by a comprehensive analysis of monetary policy, fiscal development, the performance of the country's financial

81

institutions, rural credit facilities, cooperatives, pricing policy and the viability and activities of the specific parastatals in these fields.

289 **Cereals policy reform in the Sahel: Burkina Faso.**
Paris: OECD, 1986. 129p.

A report detailing the grain-marketing system in Burkina Faso which incorporated the major reforms suggested by an earlier (1977) report which posed three alternatives: retaining the status quo between the rôle of private traders and state marketing activities; a tighter centralization in state hands as in the Mali model; and a free-trade system accompanied by structural improvements. The latter had been the favoured option, and despite criticism about the excessive rôle played by non-nationals in private trade it had been implemented in its totality by the government. The report indicates that this did not lead to marketing improvements, and indeed unsatisfactory results had been recorded.

290 **The dynamics of grain marketing in Burkina Faso.**
Jacqueline R. Sherman, Kenneth H. Shapiro, Elon Gilbert. Ann Arbor, Michigan: University of Michigan Center for Research on Economic Development, 1987. 2 vols.

This massive examination of private-sector grain marketing in Burkina Faso was carried out as part of the USAID programme in the country. Three studies were mounted concurrently: the conduct of consumers and food sellers in big cities; producer marketing behaviour in five villages using farm management approaches; and marketing networks in the entire country.

291 **The efficiency of private channels in the distribution of cereals in Burkina Faso.**
Mahir Saul. In: *Production and autonomy: anthropological studies and critiques of development*, edited by John W. Bennett, John R. Bowen. Lanham, Maryland: University Press of America, 1988, p. 105-23.

A critical analysis of private cereal distribution networks in Burkina Faso, aimed at correcting assumptions that these are more efficient than the better-known poor performance of State Marketing Boards. The author suggests that the dichotomy between private and state distribution systems is not very sharp, especially if one takes into account the capital limitations of private traders, social costs, the relative inefficiency of both systems, and the storage and transportation anomalies of the private sector. The author asserts that private trade is 'not free of inefficiencies . . . [does] not have the flexibility to respond to localized, but acute and serious shortages . . . [nor does it] achieve minimum costs in the distribution of grains' (p. 103).

292 **Employment in rural industries in eastern Upper Volta.**
David Wilcock, Enyinna Chuta. *International Labour Review* (Geneva), vol. 121, no. 4 (Aug. 1982), p. 455-68.

Summary of the findings of a 1980 survey of small-scale retail, manufacturing and service enterprises in 637 villages in eastern Burkina Faso, the bulk of which were individually or family-owned. The study assessed employment sources, the technology utilized and management practices. Most employed no machinery and were essentially open-air stalls, explaining the low start-up capital needed for activities traditionally seen as high-capital ventures (675,544 CFAF for grain-milling; 408,077 CFAF for welding [CFAF = Communauté Financière Africain francs]). The survey suggested that many enterprises were of marginal profitability, established without cost–benefit analyses or market assessments, while others should be assisted in re-orientation or expansion. For fuller details on the survey see David Wilcock, *Rural small-scale enterprises in eastern Upper Volta: survey results* (East Lansing, Michigan: Michigan State University, 1981. 141p. [African Rural Economy Working Paper no. 38]).

293 **Entreprises et entrepreneurs du Burkina Faso: vers une lecture anthropologique de l'entreprise africaine.** (Businesses and entrepreneurs in Burkina Faso: towards an anthropological interpretation of African business.)
Pascal Labazée. Paris: Karthala, 1988. 274p.

A fascinating, widely acclaimed study by an economic anthropologist of the conflicting interests of private enterprise in Burkina Faso and the administration which imposes rules on trade in the country. Labazée argues that, essentially, the route to economic success lies in using social and family networks to access both the administration and the business world. Labazée develops a typology of entrepreneurs based on their self-identification, the mode of acquisition of their original wealth, and style of directing their current enterprises. He then analyses the kinds of economic and structural problems constraining their further development. The book concludes with a survey of the kinds of confusion and uncertainty triggered by the rise to power of Thomas Sankara and his 'anti-bourgeois' diatribes and policies.

294 **L'état voltaïque et les sociétés face au développement.** (The Voltaic state and societies facing development.)
Paul Nikyéma. *Revue Juridique et Politique* (Paris), vol. 32, no. 1 (Jan.-March 1978), p. 97-122.

An article by the director of legislation and documentation at the Ministry of Justice outlining the reasons for state intervention in the economy and the creation of mixed societies. The article supplies specific details of the companies involved and their capitalization.

295 **Haute-Volta: forces et faiblesses de l'économie.** (Upper Volta: strengths and weaknesses of the economy.)
Jacques Belotteau. *Afrique Contemporaine* (Paris), no. 124 (Nov.-Dec. 1982), p. 11-21.

A compact but comprehensive overview of all aspects of the Voltaic economy, levels of agrarian and mining production, and the balance of trade for the period 1974-81, illustrated by twelve tables. For a compendium of economic statistics, see 'Haute-Volta' (Upper Volta) in *L'économie des pays d'Afrique Noire* (The economy of the countries of Black Africa) (Paris: Ediafric, 1987. 2nd ed.). For earlier years, see also the voluminous *L'économie voltaïque* (The Voltaic economy) (Paris: Ediafric, 1971. 198p.). For the most recent economic overview, see *Analyse de la situation économique et financière du Burkina Faso de 1983-1989 et perspectives* (An analysis of the economic and financial situation in Burkina Faso 1983-89 and its prospects) (Ouagadougou: Front Populaire, 1990. 46p.).

## The Economy, Trade and Commerce

296 **How relevant is flexible specialization in Burkina Faso?**
Meine Pieter Van Dijk. *IDS Bulletin* (Brighton), vol. 23, no. 3 (July 1992), p. 45-50.

Based on 1991 data from Ouagadougou, this study puts into practice the concept of flexible specialization, and examines its relevance in Burkina Faso. The informal sector of Ouagadoudou showed a tremendous growth in the 1980s, with a significant percentage of the population now involved in the informal economy, but only a small number of these succeed in making the transition into the formal industrial sector. Large numbers are marginalized entrepreneurs. See also the same author's 'Burkina Faso: modern medium scale enterprises' in *Industrialization in the Third World: the need for alternative strategies*, edited by Meine Pieter Van Dijk, H. Secher (London: Frank Cass, 1992, p. 102-23.

297 **The impact of self-imposed adjustment: the case of Burkina Faso, 1983-1989.**
Kimseyinga Savadogo, Claude Wetta. Florence, Italy: Innocenti Occasional Papers, 1990. 49p. (Structural Adjustment in Africa series, no. 15).

An analysis of Burkina Faso's economic self-adjustment after the 1983 revolution, examining both its successes and its failures. In many fields advances were scored but overall these were significant only when compared to the previous stagnant era (1960-83). As the authors note, 'until farm technology and industrial management are improved, the production of food and industrial output will remain unstable and social welfare will suffer' (p. 45).

298 **Mobilization of the private sector in Burkina Faso.**
Elliott Berg, Thérèse Belot. Ouagadougou: Ministry of the Plan, 1985. 21p. bibliog.

A report prepared for the Ministry of the Plan outlining the main features of the Burkinabe economy, and incorporating specific policy recommendations as to how to motivate the private sector. The private sector employed 95 per cent of salaried Burkinabe, including 80 per cent of those in manufacturing, and 95 per cent of those in trade and transport.

299 **The organization of a West African grain market.**
Mahir Saul. *American Anthropologist* (Washington), vol. 89, no. 1 (1987), p. 74-95.

A description of the origins and expansion of the grain market and trade from colonial days to the contemporary era. Collection and distribution is by a large network of small agents acting on behalf of major traders. Competition is restricted since the traders work with little capital while producers need immediate cash and have little option to hold out. Access by farmers to capital resources would thus strengthen their rôle in the grain market. See also Mahir Saul, 'Development of the grain market and merchants in Burkina Faso', *Journal of Modern African Studies* (London) vol. 24, no. 1 (March 1986), p. 127-53.

# The Economy, Trade and Commerce

300 **Premier plan quinquennal de développement populaire 1986-1990.** (First five-year plan for popular development 1986-90.)
Ouagadougou: Ministère de la Planification et du Développement Populaire, 1988. 2 vols.

The most comprehensive survey of the Burkinabe economy to date, with a sector-by-sector analytical and statistical overview. For former development plans, see 'Haute-Volta: le plan quinquennal 1977-1981' (Upper Volta: the five-year plan 1977-1981), *Afrique Industrie* (Paris), no. 218 (Nov. 1980), p. 60-75; and 'Le premier plan de développement de la Haute-Volta, 1967-70' (The first development plan of Upper Volta, 1967-70), *Industries et Travaux d'Outre Mer* (Paris), (Oct. 1967), p. 873-80.

301 **Structures et perspectives de l'artisanat et de la petite industrie du Sud-ouest de la Haute-Volta.** (Structures and prospects for artisan enterprise and small-scale industry in southwest Upper Volta.)
Dorothée Fiedler (et al.). Berlin: Institut Allemand de Développement, 1978. 253p.

A minutely detailed study of small-scale industry and artisan enterprise in southeast Burkina Faso, using 1975 as the base-line. The work includes a critique of government policy and suggestions regarding both the policy changes and the legislation needed to improve the situation.

302 **La substitution des céréales locales par les céréales importées: la consommation alimentaire des ménages à Ouagadougou.** (The substitution of local cereals by imported cereals: food consumption in Ouagadougou households.)
Thomas A. Reardon, Taladidia Thiombiano, Christopher L. Delgado. Ouagadougou: Université de Ouagadougou, Centre d'Etudes, de Documentation et de Recherches Economiques et Sociales, 1988. 65p. bibliog.

A study of the reasons for the inelasticity of demand for imported grains such as rice. The high price of imports will not change the eating habits of the working population who regard them as convenience foods, while to those who can shift to less expensive grains, rice is attractive as part of their new 'Western' lifestyle.

303 **Survey report on road and city planning related to the Tambao Manganese Mine project.**
Tokyo: Japanese International Cooperation Agency, 1976. 116p.

The report of a Japanese mission to Burkina Faso in March 1976 which surveyed the facilities needed to develop the Tambao manganese mines, the Tambao township itself, and the trunk road between Dori and Tambao, including a cost-analysis of all the work required.

304 **Traders and marketing boards in Upper Volta: ten years of state intervention in agricultural marketing.**
L. Filippi-Wilhelm.   In: *Marketing boards in tropical Africa*, edited by Kwame Arhin (et al.).   London: Kegan Paul, 1985, p. 120-48.

An assessment of the positive and negative aspects of marketing boards and purchasing agents in the marketing of agricultural produce, especially of grains.

# Conservation, Drought and Ecology

305 **Agrométéorologie et développement des régions arides et semi-arides.**
(Agrometeorology and development in arid and semi-arid regions.)
Charles Baldy. Paris: Institut National de la Recherche
Agronomique, 1985. 114p. bibliog.
A survey of the relationship between agrometeorology and development in three
countries – Burkina Faso, Tunisia and Lebanon – and the modification over time of the
climate in all three as a result of overpopulation, soil degradation and the resultant
desertification.

306 **Coping with household-level food insecurity in drought-affected areas of
Burkina Faso.**
Thomas Reardon, Peter Matlon, Christopher Delgado. *World
Development* (Oxford), vol. 16, no. 9 (Sept. 1988), p. 1065-74. bibliog.
An examination, by three food-policy experts, of the strategies adopted by rural
households in Burkina Faso to ensure food security. One policy has been a greater
reliance on income derived from non-crop sources: fully three-quarters of household
income in the Sahel region, and half of income in the Sudanic belt is no longer
dependent upon staple crops.

307 **La déroute d'un système vivrier au Burkina: agriculture extensive et
baisse de production.** (The ruin of a food crop system in Burkina:
extensive agriculture and lowered produce.)
Jean-Yves Marchal. *Etudes Rurales* (Paris), vol. 99/100 (1985),
p. 265-80.
A demonstration (which includes an English summary) of the progressive degradation
of soil and the desertification of northern Burkina Faso during recent decades as a
result of permanent intensive agriculture as opposed to prior patterns of intermittent
agriculture. Other side-effects have been an atomization of population groups,
decreased agrarian output and increased man-hours needed to produce this output. See

also the same author's 'Facteurs climatiques limitants et calamités agricoles en regions de savane: Yatenga' (Limiting climatic factors and agricultural calamities in grassland regions: Yatenga), *Herodote* (Paris), vol. 24, no. 1 (1982), p. 68-94, where he argues that the natural calamities which have afflicted Burkina Faso, and Yatenga specifically (drought, desertification, famine) are only in part ecological in origin: soil degradation due to agrarian overpopulation has played an equal rôle. See also his 'The evolution of agrarian systems in Yatenga', *Africa Environment* (Dakar), vol. 2, no. 4 (1977), p. 73-86, where he argues that Yatenga's agrarian system is one which can no longer feed its inhabitants, a fact worsened after the series of disastrous droughts. Exporting manpower at a level just below its birth-rate, 'it no longer seems feasible to think of a possible development of Yatenga' (p. 85).

308 **Fiches techniques de conservation du sol.** (Technical data on soil conservation.)
Fred R. Weber, Marilyn W. Hoskins. Ouagadougou: Office de Coopération et de Développement Internationale, 1983. 112p.

Detailed and illustrated soil conservation strategies for arid Burkina Faso, produced by a team from the University of Idaho Forest, Wildlife and Range Experimental Station on contract to the Sahel Club through the US Department of Agriculture.

309 **Foodgrain disposals as early warning famine signals: a case from Burkina Faso.**
Constance McCorkle. *Disasters* (London), vol. 11, no. 4 (1987), p. 273-81. bibliog.

Based on research conducted in southern Burkina Faso during the 1983-84 drought, a variety of early warning signals of impending famine are outlined. These include sudden changes in marketing patterns, non-market-oriented exchanges, changes in dietary practice, the use of agricultural labour for pastoral tasks, and preoccupation with ideological issues. These, it is argued, are better indicators of potential disasters than the monitoring of physical processes alone.

310 **Le Sahel en lutte contre la désertification: leçons d'expérience.** (The Sahel's struggle against desertification: the lessons of experience.)
Edited by R. M. Rochette. Weikersheim, Germany: Verlag Josef Margraf, 1989. 592p.

A comprehensive survey of the encroaching desertification of the Sahel and the various strategies employed by its populations to continue securing a livelihood from its degraded soils. The collection of essays includes nine on Burkina Faso.

311 **The social impacts of planned settlement in Burkina Faso.**
Della E. McMillan. In: *Drought and hunger in Africa: denying famine a future*, edited by M. H. Glantz. Cambridge, England: Cambridge University Press, 1987, p. 297-322. bibliog.

An assessment of some of the policy prerequisites for organized relocation of farmers from degraded drought-prone areas, illustrated by the experience of Burkina Faso after the 1968-73 drought. Most such resettlements in Africa have not been successful since relief programmes have not usually been followed up with production and community development programmes subsequent to relocation of farmers.

# Agriculture and Rural Development

312 **Agrarian change and the revolution in Burkina Faso.**
Mike Speirs. *African Affairs*, vol. 90, no. 358 (Jan. 1991), p. 89-110.
A comparative study of agriculture during the régimes of Sankara and Campaore.
Although the agricultural sector is as stunted today as under Sankara, the régime is
relying on the hope of modernization which is to be achieved by the 'strengthening of
the commercial classes'. However, the author concludes that 'as long as states are
dominated by military, bureaucratic and commercial elites, the exclusion of the
smallholder peasant farmer from political power and influence represents a major
obstacle to effective agrarian change' (p. 110).

313 **Agricultural mechanization: the economics of animal draft power in
West Africa.**
William K. Jaeger. Boulder, Colorado: Westview Press, 1986. 199p.
bibliog.
An attempt to resolve conflicting evidence and contrary views on the profitability of
animal traction in semi-arid Burkina Faso where the use of farm animals has been low,
and when attempted has usually been abandoned within three to five years. The study
is based on survey data and interviews with farmers in several districts. See also Yves
Bigot, Georges Raymond, *Traction animale et motorisation en zone cotonnière
d'Afrique de l'Ouest* (Animal traction and mechanization in cotton-growing areas of
West Africa) (Montpellier, France: Cirad, 1991. 95p.).

314 **Agricultural production, social status, and intra-compound
relationships.**
Helga Vierich. In: *Understanding Africa's rural households and
farming systems*, edited by Joyce Lewinger Moock. Boulder,
Colorado: Westview Press, 1986, p. 155-65.
Vierich presents a fascinating exploration, based on fieldwork among the Bwawa and
Dagari-Dyula, of hypotheses about the cultural and organizational causes of major

variations in productivity among different farming units in Burkina Faso. The hypotheses relate to the rôle played by family composition and customs, ethnicity and social status in affecting desire for, and access to, resources, labour and land. The author concludes that different technological 'packages' are more appropriate in order to mesh with diverse cultural values that dictate levels of agrarian activity. For an analysis of two cropping systems, one significantly more efficient and intensive (among the Tengbiise) than the other (Mossi), practised by peoples where different nucleur family size may be the determining factor, see Jean-Yves Marchal, 'Lorsque l'outil ne compte plus: techniques agraires et entités sociales au Yatenga' (When tools no longer count: agricultural techniques and social groups in Yatenga), *Cahiers d'ORSTOM* (Paris), vol. 20, no. 3/4 (1984), p. 461-9. For another valuable study comparing Bwa (crop networking) and Pougouli (individualized farming) agrarian patterns, see Ousmane Nebie, 'Evolution des systèmes agraires bwa et pougoli de Po-Ouest, Burkina Faso' (The evolution of the Bwa and Pougoli agrarian systems in Po-West, Burkina Faso), *Cahiers d'Outre-mer* (Bordeaux), vol. 41, no. 163 (1988), p. 259-82. This last article has a bibliography and an English summary.

315 **Burkina Faso: the project Agro-forestier.**
Stephen D. Younger, Edouard G. Bonkoungou. In: *Successful development in Africa: case studies of projects, programs and policies*, edited by R. Bheenick (et al.). Washington, DC: The World Bank, 1989, p. 11-26.
A report on the labour-intensive technology aimed at water collection, increasing crop yields, preventing soil erosion and agricultural extension services adopted in the drought-stricken region of Yatenga, which succeeded where previous efforts, public and private, had failed.

316 **Cotton development programs in Burkina Faso, Côte d'Ivoire and Togo.**
Washington, DC: The World Bank, 1988. 126p.
Compiled by the Operations Evaluations department of the World Bank, this is a report on three cotton development programmes aimed at supporting smallholders. In each case the project objectives were achieved or surpassed. This success, which is in contrast to mediocre records of cotton development projects elsewhere, is largely due to the integrated technical, financial, marketing and research services adopted in the three countries. Burkina Faso is considered specifically in Annex 1 (p. 49-74). This work should be used in conjunction with another study which points out that cotton cultivation has been successful largely due to the fact that it has not been at the expense of self-sufficiency in foodstuffs consequent to farmers' year-round crop rotation practices (cotton, corn, millet).

317 **Determinants and effects of income diversification among farm households in Burkina Faso.**
Thomas Reardon, Christopher Delgado, Peter Matlon. *Journal of Development Studies* (London), vol. 28, no. 2 (Jan. 1992), p. 264-96. bibliog.
Based on four years of household data from three diverse agricultural zones, the authors assess the determinants and effects of household income diversification. Land constraints surprisingly did not produce diversification, although harvest shortfalls and poor conditions of trade did so.

318 **Developing new agricultural technologies for the Sahelian countries: the Burkina Faso case.**
John H. Sanders, Joseph G. Nagy, Sunder Ramaswamy. *Economic Development and Cultural Change* (Chicago), vol. 39, no. 1 (Oct. 1990), p. 1-22.

Despite substantial investment in agricultural research and in specific programmes since the 1968-73 drought, agrarian stagnation has continued throughout Africa, including ithe areas unaffected by drought. The authors offer several alternative strategies aimed at revitalizing agricultural development.

319 **Distribution of resources and products in Mossi households.**
Della E. McMillan. In: *Food in sub-Saharan Africa*, edited by Art Hansen, Della E. McMillan. Boulder, Colorado: Lynne Rienner, 1986, p. 260-73.

McMillan argues that failure to understand the complex patterning of distribution between households limits appreciation of the constraints on increased food production in Burkina Faso. See also Mahir Saul, 'Consumption and intra-household patterns among the southern Bobo of Burkina Faso' in *The social economy of consumption*, edited by Henry Rutz, Benjamin Orlove (Lanham, Maryland: University Press of America, 1987, p. 349-78. bibliog.).

320 **Donor investment preference, class formation and existential development: articulation of production relations in Burkina Faso.**
Stephen P. Reyna. In: *Anthropology and rural development in West Africa*, edited by Michael M. Horowitz, Thomas M. Painter. Boulder, Colorado: Westview Press, 1986, p. 223-47.

An exploration of the relationship between external investments and class formation in Burkina Faso. Investments are seen as enhancing the process of 'dual class formation, which in turn creates four social categories of opportunity' (p. 246) with negative implications. In a similar vein is Stephen P. Reyna's 'Dual class formation and agrarian underdevelopment: an analysis of the articulation of production relations in Upper Volta', *Canadian Journal of African Studies* (Montreal), vol. 17, no. 2 (1983), p. 211-33. bibliog. The latter argues that foreign investments, manifestations of core colonial and neo-colonial tactics all affect control of land in Burkina Faso. See also Stephen P. Reyna, 'Investing in inequality: class formation in Upper Volta' in *Power and poverty: development and development projects in the Third World*, edited by Donald W. Atwood (et al.) (Boulder, Colorado: Westview Press, 1988, p. 119-33).

321 **Economic policies and agricultural performance: the case of Burkina Faso, 1960-1983.**
Jacques Lecaillon, Christian Morrisson. Paris: OECD, 1985. 158p. bibliog.

Exhaustive sector-by-sector study of the relationship between agricultural performance and macro-economic political policies and structures in Burkina Faso, and the constraints on agricultural development. The work concludes that the major constraints – rapid population growth and climatic or soil conditions – can never be eliminated, and that unless serious road-building commences regional imbalances and underdevelopment will not be alleviated. The authors also contend that the policies pursued since 1973 had been more favourable to farmers than those in force between 1960 and 1973.

322 **Entraide villageoise et développement: groupements paysans au Burkina Faso.** (Village mutual aid and development: rural groupings in Burkina Faso.)
Bernard Ledea Ouedraogo. Paris: Harmattan, 1990. 177p.

A study of Mossi temporary *naam* mutual-aid associations, set up from time immemorial to tackle agricultural and other tasks too onerous for one community alone. The associations have in recent decades proliferated throughout the country: several are pinpointed for specific attention, and their concrete developmental achievements are assessed.

323 **Farming systems research on the northern Mossi plateau.**
Jan T. Broekhuyse, Andrea M. Allen. *Human Organization* (Oklahoma City), vol. 47, no. 4 (Winter 1988), p. 330-42. bibliog.

An analysis of the design, results and long-term prospects of a specific Dutch project funded in Burkina Faso along 'French' lines, that is, involving a much longer time-scale and encompassing a larger unit than is common for British- or US-funded projects. Technological innovations (such as fertilizer, animal traction and tied ridges) and supporting structures (credit and management facilities) were introduced only after intensive study of current and past systems of agriculture, thus linking short-term benefits for farmers with long-term outcomes for society.

324 **Les inégalités de développement régional au Burkina Faso.** (The inequalities of regional development in Burkina Faso.)
K. Ernest Ilboudo. Ouagadougou: Université de Ouagadougou, Centre d'Etudes, de Documentation et de Recherches Economiques et Sociales, 1987. 140p. bibliog.

An important and exhaustive study of Burkina Faso's regional inequalities, a function of unequal distribution of natural resources, climatological and soil differences, and differential access to education by youth, all of which have resulted in distorted socio-economic development and disparities among its peoples. For examples from the southern Lobi and Bwa districts, see Georges Savonnet, 'Inégalités de développement et organisation sociale' (Unequal development and social organization), *Cahiers d'ORSTOM* (Paris), vol. 13, no. 1 (1976), p. 23-40. This last has an English summary.

325 **Livestock versus foodgrain production in southeast Upper Volta: a resource allocation analysis.**
Christopher L. Delgado. Ann Arbor: University of Michigan Center for Research on Economic Developoment, 1979, 427p.

A report to USAID, based on prolonged fieldwork, challenging conventional wisdom of farmers' resistance to mixed farming, and urging the integration of livestock in existing farms to maximize farmer profits. The major labour constraints are at harvest time when livestock would lose mobility to prevent crop damage. For an extension of the argument, see the same author's 'The changing economic context of mixed farming in savanna West Africa: a conceptual framework applied to Burkina Faso', *Quarterly Journal of International Agriculture* (London), vol. 28, no. 3/4 (1989), p. 351-64.

Agriculture and Rural Development

326  **Money and land tenure as factors in farm size differentiations in Burkina Faso.**
Mahir Saul.  In: *Land and society in contemporary Africa*, edited by R. E. Downs, S. P. Reyna.  Hanover, New Hampshire: University of New England Press, 1988, p. 243-79. bibliog.
A study of the factors that led to the emergence of large-scale farmers in Burkina Faso, a 'capitalist phenomenon' that the author argues has not altered 'the main features of an old regime which negates the possibility of commoditization in farmland' (p. 245).

327  **Les paysages agraires de Haute-Volta: analyse structurale par la méthode graphique.** (The agrarian landscapes of Upper Volta: a graphic structural analysis.)
Monique Marchal.  Paris: ORSTOM, 1983. 115p. maps. bibliog.
Comprehensive graphic cartographical inventory of Burkina Faso's agricultural landscape.  For the use of satellite pictures, superimposed on ethnic maps to give better contrast of different agrarian patterns, see Eric Lambin, 'L'apport de la télédetection dans l'étude des systèmes agraires d'Afrique: Burkina Faso' (The use of remote sensing in the study of agrarian systems in Africa: Burkina Faso), *Africa* (London), vol. 58, no. 3 (1988), p. 337-52. This last is accompanied by an English summary.

328  **State policies on agriculture and food production in Burkina Faso 1960-1983.**
T. Thiombiano.  In: *The state and agriculture in Africa*, edited by Thandika P. Mkandawire, Naceur Bourenane.  London: Codesria, 1987, p. 243-71.
A harsh neo-Marxist survey of economic conditions in Burkina Faso, and the policies of the country's successive governments, civil, military, capitalist or Marxist. The author concludes that irrespective of the kind of régime in office, state intervention in the economy 'has been based on no coherent strategy' despite intermittent affirmations of the priority of agriculture and rural areas. The specific agrarian sector to serve the driving force of the economy has never been identified or pinpointed: in a country with regions unequally endowed with natural resources and marked by acute regional disparities, no effort has been made at a redistribution of wealth, nor has the possibility of regional specialization even been raised, with the state 'content to let internationalist capitalist groups find a solution to this issue'. According to Thiombiano, social revolutions are likely to erupt in the absence of leadership since the 'bourgeoisie was unable to develop the productive forces indispensible for its own survival . . . incompatible with the aspirations of the country's emergent youth, especially literate urban youth' (p. 268).

329  **Tiogo, étude géographique d'un terroir Iéla (Haute-Volta).**
(Tiogo, a geographical study of an Iela territory.)
Henri Barral.  Paris: Mouton, 1968. 72p. bibliog.
A significant multifaceted study of the small village of Tiogo on the Koudougou–Dedougou road, illustrating the reasons for its poverty and economic marginalization, and the depressed levels of agrarian activity in many other parts of Burkina Faso. Notwithstanding the availability of uncultivated land, the low number of active farmers at Tiogo (20 per cent of the total inhabitants), their poor health, minimal resources and

few mechanized means of ploughing assure meagre results. To this can be added a spirit of individualism which has replaced previous collective cultivation patterns, thus adding to the problems of agriculture.

330 **Work parties, wages, and accumulation in a Voltaic village.**
Mahir Saul. *American Ethnologist* (Washington, DC), vol. 10, no. 1 (Feb. 1983), p. 77-96.

An attempt to determine the significance of labour flows between African farming units, in order to assess the possibilities of accumulation and its implications for local-level stratification. Three forms of labour are compared: household, wage and cooperative.

331 **'You can't eat cotton': cash crops and the cereal code of honor in Burkina Faso.**
Constance M. McCorkle. In: *Production and autonomy: anthropological studies and critiques of development*, edited by John W. Bennett, John R. Bowen. Lanham, Maryland: University Press of America, 1988, p. 87-103.

Critical overview of development programmes stressing maximization of cotton cash-crop farming. The shift from traditional subsistence crop farming, even if it results in increased incomes in good years, produces major subsistence shortfalls and hardships in the negative ecological conditions that periodically afflict Sahel countries.

**Creating hunger: labor and agricultural policies in southern Mossi, 1919-1940.**
*See* item no. 127.

# Communications

332  **Enclavement et mobilité en Afrique occidentale: l'exemple du Burkina Faso.** (Encirclement and mobility in West Africa: the example of Burkina Faso.)
Gabriel Wackermann. *Afrique Contemporaine* (Paris), no. 140 (Oct.-Dec. 1986), p. 24-39. bibliog.
Comprehensive survey of the constraints of Burkina Faso's land-locked location, transport options and levels of commercial and passenger usage. The only asset the country has is the 1,145-kilometre Ouagadougou–Abidjan railroad, but the latter is slow and poorly maintained. Road options include the Ouagdougou–Lomé (Togo) and Ouagadougou–Accra (Ghana) links. Air links are poor, and many parts of the country are completely isolated without any regular mode of transport. For a country which has to import the bulk of its needs, developing an efficient and reliable communications network is a vital necessity.

333  **Enquête transport routier.** (Inquiry into road transport.)
Ouagadougou: Institut National de la Statistique et de la Démographie, 1988. 107p.
Inventory of traffic levels and traffic loads on each road in the country, by type of vehicle using it and time of travel. An equally valuable publication that puts Burkina Faso's problems of communication within a socio-economic framework is *Transports routiers et développement socio-économique en Haute-Volta: rapports d'enquêtes* (Road transport and socio-economic development in Upper Volta: reports of the enquiry) (Ouagadougou: Université de Ouagadougou Groupe d'Etudes et de Recherches 'Transport et Développement', 1984. 184p.).

# Communications

334 **La route Ouagadougou–Bobo-Dioulasso.** (The Ouagadougou–Bobo-Dioulasso road.)
Bernard Guerin. *Cahiers d'Outre-mer* (Bordeaux), no. 145 (Jan.-March 1984), p. 5-32.

A survey of the Ouagadougou–Bobo-Dioulasso road which traverses the Volta savannah lands linking the country's two main cities. In contrast to other areas of Burkina Faso, new villages have not sprung up along the road, nor have the locations of dwellings or migration patterns been much affected by the existence of the road. Mossi life is hierarchically patterned and relocation for most is inconceivable. For this reason the long road is relatively little used, and neither covers its maintenance costs nor produces economic or agrarian development, a situation compounded by the fact that there are very few vehicles in the country.

335 **Les voies de communications au Burkina Faso.** (Means of communication in Burkina Faso.)
Patrice Cosaert. *Cahiers d'Outre-mer* (Bordeaux), vol. 43, no. 169 (1990), p. 53-76.

A study of the various communications options available for more effectively opening up the country, a major priority of the régime. The inauguration of a fully paved Ouagadougou–Lomé (Togo) road, currently under increasing use, has caused a decline in the use of the old Ouagadougou–Abidjan (Côte d'Ivoire) railway, which was previously the main communication route.

# The Arts

## Performing arts

336 **Bendrologie et littérature culturelle des Mossé. Introduction à la littérature non-écrite d'Afrique: littérature orale, langue de tam-tams, messages des masques et des danses.** (Bendrology and the cultural literature of the Mossi. Introduction to the non-written literature of Africa: oral literature, tam-tam language, and the messages conveyed by masks and dances.)
Frédéric Titinga Pacéré. Ouagadougou: Titinga Pacéré, 1987. 6 vols.
This massive and highly original overview of 'bendrologie' (defined as the scientific study of Bendre drums) was written by a prolific Burkinabe author of works spanning a dazzling variety of fields, and the 1982 winner of the African Grand Prize for Literature. The work is a collection of songs, oral tradition, and analysis of the kinds of drums and other musical instruments used in Mossi society, their rôle, and the messages which they convey.

337 **Chants d'enfants mossi.** (The songs of Mossi children.)
Oger Kaboré. *Journal des Africanistes* (Paris), vol. 51, no. 1/2 (1981), p. 183-200.
From infancy to adolescence Mossi children play games accompanied by songs, and associate songs and rhythms with various forms of activity. The author analyses the content, form and symbolic message in a variety of such songs. An English summary is supplied.

338 **Five West African film makers on their films.**
Françoise Pfaff. *Issue* (Atlanta), vol. 20, no. 2 (1992), p. 31-7.
One of the few articles in English on Francophone African film makers, this essay includes a discussion of the Burkinabe Gaston Kabore and Idrissa Ouedraogo. See also

97

The Arts. Performing arts

N. Schmidt, 'Publications on African film: focus on Burkina Faso and Nigeria', *African Book Publishing Record* (London), vol. 16, no. 3 (1990), p. 153-6.

339  **La Haute-Volta et le cinéma.** (Upper Volta and the cinema.)
Victor Bachy.  Paris: Harmattan, 1983. 87p. bibliog.

Until 1969 there were only six cinemas in Upper Volta. In 1970 the cinemas were nationalized and by the mid-1980s there were already seventeen cinemas, record attendance, and a cinematographic tradition rivalling that in more developed countries. This work is an outline of Burkinabe cinematography, cinemas and cinema attendance from its origins to the 1980s, followed by biographical sketches of Burkinabe directors, and a listing of their films.

340  **Les instruments de musique du pays cerma (guin), sud-ouest du Burkina Faso.** (Musical instruments of the Cerma (Guin) country, southwest of Burkina Faso.)
Etienne Yarmon Soma.  *Anthropos* (Fribourg), vol. 83, no. 4/6 (1988), p. 469-83.

An illustrated description (with English summary) of Guin musical instruments.

341  **Musique traditionnelle de l'Afrique noire: Haute Volta.** (Traditional music of Black Africa: Upper Volta.)
Chantal Nourrit, Bill Pruitt.  Paris: Radio France Internationale, 1978. 67p.

An introductory essay on the music of the Mossi and other groups in Burkina Faso, followed by a detailed listing of all records of Burkinabe music issued to that date, indexed by ethnic group.

342  **Pièces théâtrales du Burkina.** (Plays of Burkina.)
Ouagadougou: Ministère de l'Information et de la Culture, 1983. 157p.

Three plays by Moussa Théophile Sowie, Issa Nikiéma Tinga and Martin Zongo. For another volume of two plays, see Jacques Prosper Bazie, *Théâtre* (Ouagadougou: Ministère de la Culture, 1986. 86p.).

343  **La poésie des griots.** (The poetry of the griots.)
Frédéric Titinga Pacéré.  Paris: Silex, 1983. 2nd ed. 133p.

Contains full texts of the songs of Burkina Faso's *griots* [poets and musicians who are guardians of the oral tradition].

344  **Théâtre et développement au Burkina Faso.** (Theatre and development in Burkina Faso.)
Jean-Pierre Guingané.  *Revue d'Histoire du Théâtre* (Paris), vol. 40, no. 4 (1988), p. 361-73.

A discussion of the rôle of theatre in spearheading the populist transformation of Burkina Faso. See also Jean-Claude Ki, 'Dix ans de théâtre: 1979-1989' (Ten years of theatre), *Notre Librairie* (Paris), no. 101 (1990), p. 72-5.

# Sculpture and masks

345 **Art Nioniosi.** (Nyonyosi art.)
Annemarie Schweeger-Hefel. *Journal des Africanistes* (Paris), vol. 36, no. 2 (1966), p. 251-332. bibliog.

Definitive study, by a highly respected scholar, of the religious art, masks, ceremonies and the strikingly tall sculpture of the Kurumba. Numerous plates accompany the study. See also the author's *Steinskulpturen der Nyonyosi aus Ober-Volta* (Stone sculptures of the Nyonyosi of Upper Volta) (Munich, Germany: Fred Jahn, 1981. 128p.); *Masken und Mythen, Sozialstrukturen der Nyonyosi und Silomse in Obervolta* (Masks and myths, social structures of the Nyonyosi and Silomse of Upper Volta) (Vienna: A. Schendl, 1980. 480p); and 'Steinskulpturen und Masken der Nyonyosi in Burkina Faso' (Stone sculptures and masks of the Nyonyosi in Burkina Faso) in *Ethnologies: hommage à Marcel Griaule* (Ethnic groups: tribute to Marcel Griaule), edited by Solange Ganay (et al.) (Paris: Hermann, 1987, p. 231-87).

346 **Bronzes de Ouagadougou.** (The bronzes of Ouagadougou.)
Marilyn W. Hoskins, Louise Charbonneau. Ouagadougou: Société Africaine des Affaires Culturelles, 1976. 56p. bibliog.

Written in both English and French, this work describes and illustrates the famous Burkinabe bronze artwork.

347 **The Dodo masquerade of Burkina Faso.**
Priscilla Baird Hinckley. *African Arts* (Los Angeles), vol. 19, no. 2 (Feb. 1986), p. 74-7.

The author describes the Dodo masquerade of Ouagadougou, a children's play activity which has become 'a means by which youths express their new sense of being powerful up-to-date Africans' (p. 74). Introduced by Hausa traders in the mid-nineteenth century, the ceremony has undergone significant change since then.

348 **The Dogon of Mali and Upper Volta.**
Christopher D. Roy. Munich, Germany: Fred Jahn, 1983. 60p. bibliog.

A study, in German and English, of the art of the Dogon community found in both Burkina Faso and Mali along the scenic Bandiagara escarpment. The book is a collection of twenty-three black-and-white plates of Dogon wood-carvings accompanied by an explanation of their diverse functions. These include their use as physical supports for the spiritual forces released by death.

349 **Forme et signification des masques mossi.** (Structure and meaning of Mossi masks.)
Christopher D. Roy. *Art d'Afrique Noire* (Paris), no. 48 (Winter 1983), p. 9-23.

A description of the manufacture, significance and utilization of Mossi masks, supported by photographs and an English summary.

The Arts. Sculpture and masks

350 **Haute-Volta.** (Upper Volta.)
Henri Kamer. Brussels: A. De Rache, 1973. 179p.
With text in both English and French and illustrated by 113 mostly black-and-white
plates this is the official catalogue of an exhibition of Burkinabe art that took place
during September 1973 in Brussels. See also another catalogue of an exhibition held in
New York: Norman Skougstad, *Traditional sculpture from Upper Volta* (New York:
The African American Institute, 1978. 43p.).

351 **Kunst und Religion der Lobi.** (Art and religion of the Lobi.)
Piet Meyer. Zurich, Switzerland: Museum Rietberg, 1981. 184p.
bibliog.
A summary of Lobi cosmology and religious beliefs, illustrated by photographs (some
in colour) of the masks and other wood-carvings used in their various rites. See also
François Warin, 'La statuaire Lobi: question de style' (Lobi statues: a question of
style), *L'Art d'Afrique Noire* (Arnouville), vol. 69 (1989), p. 11-21; Jean Dominique
Rey, *Les Lobi* (The Lobi) (Paris: Galerie Jacques Kerchache, 1974. 61p.); R. Some,
'Les bétibé: art et pouvoir chez les Lobi et les Dagara du sud-ouest du Burkina Faso'
(The Bétibé: art and power among the Lobi and Dagara in southwest Burkina Faso) in
*Séminaire de recherche*, edited by L. Perrois, C. F. Bandez. (Paris: ORSTOM, 1989,
p. 137-51).

352 **Man and his vision: the traditional wood sculpture of Burkina Faso.**
Esther A. Dagan. Montreal, Canada: Galerie Amrad, 1987. 64p.
bibliog.
The catalogue of an exhibition held at the Galerie Amrad, describing Burkinabe
traditional arts, zoomorphic motifs and their symbolism, rituals and dances, different
kinds of masks and their purposes, and musical instruments. The text is in both English
and French.

353 **Les masques dans la société marka de Fobiri et ses environs.** (The masks
in the Marka society of Fobiri and its surroundings.)
Domba Blegna. Stuttgart, Germany: F. Steiner, 1990. 262p. bibliog.
A study of the the rôle of masks, and their variety in the Marka society of Fobiri.

354 **Mossi chiefs' figures.**
Christopher D. Roy. *African Arts* (Los Angeles), vol. 15, no. 4 (Aug.
1982), p. 52-9.
A description of the wooden figures, often male and sometimes of an animal or bird,
carved as posts to stand at each side of the entrances to chiefly compounds. Some serve
decorative purposes, but others are ancestral figures from former funeral processions.

355 **Mossi dolls.**
Christopher D. Roy. *African Arts* (Los Angeles), vol. 14, no. 4 (Aug.
1981), p. 47-51. bibliog.
Description of the manufacture, variety and function of Mossi dolls, 'the most
frequently and most widely represented in American and European collections'
(p. 47). See also Ladislas Segy, 'The Mossi doll: an archetypal fertility symbol', *Tribus*

(Stuttgart), vol. 21, no. 1 (1972), p. 35-68; and Suzanne Lallemand, 'Symbolisme des poupées et acceptation de la maternité chez les Mossi' (The symbolism of dolls and the acceptance of maternity among the Mossi), *Objets et Mondes* (Paris), vol. 13, no. 4 (1973), p. 235-46.

356  **Mossi zazaido.**
Christopher D. Roy.  *African Arts* (Los Angeles), vol. 13, no. 3 (May 1980), p. 42-7.
A study of Mossi zoomorphic headcrests used in secular and traditional religious ceremonies.

357  **The spread of mask styles in the Black Volta basin.**
Christopher D. Roy.  *African Arts* (Los Angeles), vol. 20, no. 4 (1987), p. 40-7. bibliog.
Description of the kinds of masks and their significance in Burkina Faso, 'a land inhabited by two races of beings – spirits and men. Spirits are made visible by masks . . .' (p. 40).

358  **Street nativities in Ouagadougou.**
Priscilla Hinckley.  *African Arts* (Los Angeles). vol. 16, no. 3 (May 1983), p. 47-9.
A description of the spread in Ouagadougou of a new art form, the Christmas crèche street nativity. Made of mud bricks and a peaked roof set against a wall, they are painted white and bear a Christmas greeting. More sophisticated models are illustrated with colour photographs.

**Les Bobo. Nature et fonctions des masques.** (The Bobo. The nature and functions of masks.)
*See* item no. 104.

# Ceramic arts, textiles and baskets

359  **Artisanats traditionnels, Haute-Volta.** (Traditional activities of artisans, Upper Volta.)
Jocelyne Etienne-Nugué.  Dakar: Institut Culturel Africain, 1982. 216p. bibliog.
This extremely comprehensive survey is profusely illustrated with 340 black-and-white and 22 colour photographs, of the traditional work of artisans in Burkina Faso. These include leather work, pottery, textiles, wood, bronze and copperwork.

360 **Gurunsi basketry and pottery.**
Fred T. Smith. *African Arts* (Los Angeles), vol 12, no. 1 (Nov. 1978), p. 78-81. bibliog.

A description of basketry and pottery among the Gurunsi. See also Herta Haselberger, 'Bemerkungen zum Kunsthandwerk in der Republik Haute Volta' (Some remarks on artistic handicrafts in the Republic of Upper Volta), *Zeitung für Ethnologie* (Brunswick, New Jersey), vol. 94, no. 2 (1969), p. 171-246.

361 **Mossi weaving.**
Christopher D. Roy. *African Arts* (Los Angeles), vol. 15, no. 3 (May 1982), p. 48-53.

A detailed outline, accompanied by colour photographs, of the origins of the colourful and sophisticated cloth produced by the Yarse, that figured prominently in trade and gifts in the area now called Burkina Faso.

362 **Poterie et société chez les Nuna de Tierkou.** (Pottery and society among the Nuna of Tierko.)
Kouame Emmanuel Banaon. Stuttgart, Germany: F. Steiner, 1990. 186p. bibliog.

A comprehensive work with a multitude of illustrations of Nuna pottery and an examination of its rôle in their social life. For a discussion of the sacred pottery of the Lobi see K. Schneider, 'Sakrale Topferei der Lobi in Burkina Faso' (Sacred pottery of the Lobi in Burkina Faso), *Paideuma* (Frankfurt), vol. 32 (1986), p. 207-38.

# Folklore

363 **Contes du Sahel.** (Folktales of the Sahel.)
Gaston Canu. Paris: Conseil International de la Langue Française, 1975. 138p.

Folklore and fables from Mossi and other Burkinabe ethnic groups, translated into French.

364 **L'enfant, sujet du conte.** (The child, subject of folktales.)
Suzy Platiel. *Journal des Africanistes* (Paris), vol. 51, no. 1/2 (1981), p. 149-82.

Platiel's important analysis of 418 folktales about children, including those yet unborn, aimed at discovering the image of the child as a social being, the rôle of the child as object of the folktale and the kinds of cultural messages transmitted to children of different gender, lineage and status regarding their future rôle in society. An English summary is included.

365 **La fille volage.** (The flighty girl.)
Suzanne Platiel. Paris: Armand Colin, 1984. 342p.
A collection of San folk-tales from Burkina Faso, preceded by an ethno-linguistic study (p. 9-49). For a reprint of folklore collected by Louis Tauxier between 1913 and 1916 and published in his seminal work, *Le Noir du Yatenga* (The Black of Yatenga), see *Contes du Burkina* (Folktales of Burkina), edited by Louis Tauxier, Doris Bonnet. (Paris: Conseil International de la Langue Français, 1985. 135p.).

366 **Histoire et contes des Mossi.** (History and folktales of the Mossi.)
Leo Frobenius. Stuttgart, Germany: Franz Steiner, 1986. 94p.
A collection of folklore and folktales (as well as oral history on the court of Ouagadougou), collected by Frobenius at the turn of the century, and only now translated from the German original.

367 **Princess of the full moon.**
Frederic Guirma. New York: Macmillan, 1970. 32p.
A folktale from Burkina Faso. See also Frederic Guirma, *Tales of Mogho: African stories from Upper Volta* (New York: Macmillan, 1971. 113p.).

368 **La princesse Yennéga et autres histoires.** (Princess Yennéga and other stories.)
Roger Bila Kabore. Paris: Edicef, 1983. 95p.
Collection of four folktales designed for a juvenile readership.

369 **Le proverbe chez les Mossi du Yatenga.** (The proverb among the Mossi of Yatenga.)
Doris Bonnet. Paris: SELAF, 193p. bibliog.
A collection of proverbs and folklore from Yatenga. An English summary is included.

370 **Towards a complex model of parenthood: two African tales.**
Michael Houseman. *Ethnologist* (New York), vol. 15, no. 4 (Nov. 1988), p. 658-77.
Two Burkinabe folktales which reveal attitudes regarding kinship, parenthood and family relationships are discussed in this article.

# Literature

371 **Adama ou la force des choses.** (Adama or the force of circumstances.)
Pierre-Claver Ilboudo. Paris: Dakar, 1987. 154p.
A French-style novel which recounts through its hero, Adama, two years of life in Ougadougou. A similar work, focusing on the country's local administration, is Noaga Kollin, *Harol camarade commandant* (Harol, commanding comrade) (Ouagadougou: Imprimerie Presses Africaines, 1977. 110p.).

372 **Jusqu'au seuil de l'irréel.** (To the threshhold of unreality.)
Amadou Kone. Abidjan: Nouvelles Editions Africaines, 1976. 143p.
A novel about sorcery by one of Burkino Faso's better-known authors. See also the
same author's *Les fresques d'Ebinto* (The frescos of Ebinto) (Paris: La Pensée
Universelle, 1972. 141p.). For other recent novels by Burkinabe authors see Jean-
Hubert Bazie, *Champ d'août* (Field of August) (Ouagadougou: Imprimerie de la
Presse Ecrite, 1986. 124p.); Etienne Sawadogo, *Contes de jadis: récits de naguère*
(Tales of long ago: stories of yesterday) (Dakar: Nouvelles Editions Africaines, 1982.
170p.).

373 **Nouvelles du Burkina.** (Short stories of Burkina.)
Patrick Ilboudo, Jacques Prosper Bazie, Faustin S. Dabira.
Ouagadougou: Ministère de l'Information et de la Culture, 1983. 105p.
An anthology of short stories by three authors. For an overview of Burkinabe
literature, see Hyacinthe Sanwidi, 'Depuis le crépuscule des temps anciens: panorama
du roman' (From the dawn of ancient times: the panorama of the novel), *Notre
Librairie* (Paris), no. 101 (1990), p. 48-54.

# Poetry

374 **Mes flèches blanches.** (My white arrows.)
Roger Nikiéma. Ouagadougou: Imprimerie Presses Africaines, 1981.
59p.
The gifted Nikiéma's third, and most widely acclaimed, volume of poetry. The other
two volumes, available from the same publisher, were *Dessein contraire* (Contrary
design) in 1967, and *L'adorable rivale* (The adorable rival) in 1970.

375 **Poésie du Burkina.** (The poetry of Burkina.)
Jacques Prosper Bazie, Bila Roger Kabore, Hamade Y. Ouedraogo.
Ouagadougou: Ministère de l'Information et de la Culture, 1983. 149p.
An anthology of Burkinabe poetry.

376 **Quand s'envolent les grues couronnées.** (When crested cranes take
flight.)
Frédéric Titinga Pacéré. Paris: P. J.Oswald, 1976. 89p.
A collection of poetry from Burkina Faso's most prolific poet and author. See also the
author's *Refrains sous le Sahel* (Refrains beneath the Sahel) (Paris, P. J. Oswald, 1976.
89p.); *Ça tire sous le Sahel* (It attracts all the Sahel) (Paris, P. J. Oswald, 1976. 64p.);
*Du lait pour une tombe* (Milk for a tomb) (Paris, Editions Silex, 1984. 90p.).

# Architecture

377 **African spaces: designs for living in Upper Volta.**
Jean-Paul Bourdier, Trinh T. Minh-ha. New York: Africana
Publishing, 1984. 231p. bibliog.
An exhaustive study of eight Gurunsi groups' space organization and architecture. An
extensive selection of photographs, diagrams and plans illustrate the text. Another
article by the same two authors illustrates the interaction between social and
architectural evolution over time of the Ko, a Gurunsi group: 'Ko architecture: a case
study from Koena, Upper Volta', *Tribus* (Stuttgart), no. 32 (1983), p. 113-25. Bourdier
and Minh-ha have also produced a study of the Lela; see 'The architecture of a Lela
compound', *African Arts* (Los Angeles), vol. 16, no. 1 (Nov. 1982), p. 68-72.

378 **Architetture voltaiche.** (Voltaic architecture.)
Fabrizio Ago. *Africa* (Rome), no. 4 (1979), p. 341-72.
Ago examines the relationship between social organization and the meaning of
architectural objects in Burkina Faso. The work concentrates on the houses of the
Bobo, and includes architectural plans and sketches of Voltaic houses, mosques and
traditional village compounds. An English summary is included.

379 **Die Burg des Elefantenjaegers: Geschichte des 'Grossen Hauses' von
Bindoute Da (Lobi, Burkina Faso).** (The castle of the elephant-hunters:
stories of 'Big Houses' by Bindoute Da.)
Klaus Schneider. Stuttgart, Germany: Franz Steiner, 1991. 72p.
A study of Lobi architecture and building styles profusely illustrated with plates
of both exteriors and interiors. For a more comprehensive overview of the dictates
of culture on traditional architectural design, see Annemarie Fiedermutz-Laun,
'Architekturforschung in Obervolta und ihre ethnologische Aussage' (Research on the
architecture in Burkina Faso and its ethnological implications), *Paideuma* (Frankfurt),
vol. 29 (1983), p. 141-220. bibliog.

## Architecture

380 **Gurunsi wall painting.**
Fred T. Smith. *African Arts* (Los Angeles), vol. 12, no. 1 (Nov. 1978), p. 78-81. bibliog.

Description of the use of Gurunsi decorative arts in the construction of compounds, which take some forty days to complete in accordance with the advice of a soothsayer. Smith notes that most wall-paintings are 'largely non-figurative, rectilinear and symmetrical'.

381 **Koumbili: semi-sunken dwellings in Upper Volta.**
Jean-Paul Bourdier, Trinh T. Minh-ha. *African Arts* (Los Angeles), vol. 16, no. 4 (Aug. 1983), p. 40-5.

This description of Kassena compound architecture found in southern Burkina Faso in the district of Po is illustrated with photographs and sketches. The authors note that 'Semi-sunken habitations form an elaborate system of defense that in the past ran through the entirety of a compact village' (p. 42). See also Honoré P. Some, 'Habitations et occupation du sol – le yir et le village dagara: l'exemple de Tobo' (Habitations and occupancy of the land – the yir and the Dagara village: the example of Tobo), *Cahiers d'Outre-mer* (Bordeaux) vol. 43, no. 169 (1990), p. 77-95.

382 **West African mud architecture.**
Eike Haberland. *African Arts* (Los Angeles), vol. 15, no. 1 (1981), p. 44-45.

A survey of mud architecture which is 'one of the most significant but least-known type of traditional African art surviving today'. See also Sergio Domian, *Architecture soudanaise: vitalité d'une tradition urbaine et monumentale* (Sudanese architecture: the vitality of an urban and monumental tradition) (Paris: Harmattan, 1989. 191p.).

# Travel and Tourism

383 **A travers l'Afrique française: du Sénégal au Cameroun par les confins libyens.** (Across French Africa: from Senegal to Cameroon by the borders of Libya.)
André Joseph Victor de Burthe d'Annelet. Paris: Firmin-Didot, 1939. 2 vols.

Accompanied by many photographs, this account describes the 1932-35 voyage of Lt. Colonel Burthe d'Annelet, sponsored by the Ministry of Colonies, the Museum of Natural History and the Academy of Colonial Sciences. Pages 270-328 of the first volume include an account of travel from Sikasso to Bobo-Dioulasso and on to Ouagadougou and Ouahigouya.

384 **Bienvenue en Haute Volta.** (Welcome to Upper Volta.)
Boulogne, France: Editions Delroisse, 1972. 128p.

Commissioned by the Upper Volta Presidency, this book, like all volumes in this series, consists mostly of colour photographs of the country. Another collection of stunning colour photographs, accompanied by a concise text on Burkina Faso's attractions is 'La Haute Volta', in *Beautés du monde: l'Afrique Occidentale* (Beauties of the world: West Africa) (Paris: Librairie Larousse, 1980, p. 1-10).

385 **Burkina Faso.**
In: *Africa on a shoestring*, edited by Geoff Crowther. Hawthorn, Australia; Berkeley, California: Lonely Planet, 1989, p. 130-40.

An overview of the country's tourist attractions, budget accommodation and restaurants. The book includes information on how to secure visas for onward travel and on 'bush-taxi' routes. Similar information is contained in three other sources: 'Burkina Faso' in *West Africa: a survival kit*, edited by Alex Newton (Berkeley, California: Lonely Planet, 1988, p. 112-30); 'Burkina Faso' in *Bright continent: a shoestring guide to sub-Saharan Africa*, edited by Susan Blumenthal (New York: Anchor Press, 1974, p. 261-74); David Brydon, *Africa overland* (Brentford, England:

## Travel and Tourism

Roger Lascelles, 1991. 2nd ed., p. 238-42). A dated, but still useful, survey of Burkina Faso's tourist potential is 'Upper Volta' in Philip M. Allen, Aaron Segal, *The traveler's Africa: a guide to the entire continent* (New York: Hopkinson and Blake, 1973, p. 671-82).

386 **Burkina Faso.**
    In: *UTA Africa Travel Guide.* Paris: UTA Airlines, 1989, p. 39-50.

Produced by the French airline with the largest number of flights to Africa, and updated every few years, the section on Burkina Faso in this glossy publication contains capsule information on the country, geography, economy and people, followed by valuable information on the country's airports, internal air-links, transport options to town, banks, hotels and their services, addresses, prices, and details of restaurants, laundry services and the country's attractions. This is a parallel text in French and English.

387 **Burkina Faso.**
    Jim Hudges, Richard Trillo. In: *West Africa: the rough guide.*
    London: Harrap-Columbus, 1990, p. 241-97.

An extremely valuable survey of Burkina Faso's tourist attractions, including hotels in all price categories, restaurants, and an index of useful addresses. There is also a basic history of the country, and a selection of recommended travel routes.

388 **Du Niger au Golfe de Guinée pars le pays de Kong et le Mossi, 1887-89.**
    (From the River Niger to the Gulf of Guinea through the country of the Kong and the Mossi, 1887-89.)
    Louis G. Binger. Paris: Musée de l'Homme, 1980. 785p.

A single-volume reprint of the classic account of Binger's explorations south of the middle Niger river. A beautifully illustrated work with 176 wooodprints and other sketches, the material on Burkina Faso is found on pages 335-513 of volume one and pages 1-60 of volume two. Binger led the last of the major European expeditions in the area, and dispelled the notion of the 'impassable' mountains of Kong. For material on northeastern Burkina Faso by another famous explorer, see Heinrich Barth, *Travels and discoveries in North and Central Africa, 1849-55* (London: Frank Cass, 1965. vol. 3, p. 190-218. translated from the German).

389 **Guide gastronomique de Ouagadougou.** (Gastronomic guide to Ouagadougou.)
    Gerhard Turbanisch. Ouagadougou: G. Turbanisch, 1988. 55p.

A list of around fifty restaurants in Ouagadougou, ranked in four classes, including information on their location, telephone number, an indication of their ambience, the type of food served, and some prices.

390 **Haute Volta.** (Upper Volta.)
    In: *Guide Ouest Africain.* (Guide to West Africa.) Paris: Diloutremer, 1965, p. 305-60.

Despite its age, this work is still invaluable because it provides information not available anywhere else. The book is much more than a tourist guide, being essentially a compendium of all kinds of data on every district and subdistrict in Upper Volta.

391 **Sub-Saharan African travel resource guide: East and West Africa.**
Louis Taussig. Oxford: Hans Zell, 1992. 288p. (Travel Resource
Guide no. 1).
A comprehensive critically annotated listing of travel guidebooks and maps, grouped
geographically and, where appropriate, by subject such as national parks or language
phrasebooks. Whenever possible there is an indication of the cost and availability of
the material. The book also lists, in directory fashion, travel bookshops; tourist office
services; sales outlets in Europe, North America and Africa for maps; important travel
magazines; outdoor pursuit clubs; and a selection of visual materials for the region.

392 **Zigzag to Timbuktu.**
Nicholas Bennet. New York: Transatlantic, 1967; London: John
Murray, 1963. 136p.
Bennet describes his impressions of a trip from Ghana through Upper Volta to Mali.

# Reference Works, Bibliographies and Research Sources

393 **Africa Research Bulletin.**
Oxford: Blackwell. 1964- . monthly.
This is the best English-language research source for Africanists, and especially for those interested in the Francophone countries. Issued monthly in two separate series, one for political, social and cultural events, and another for economic, financial and technical issues, the material is grouped by general theme and by country. The publication abstracts in lengthy form news items, reports and other data appearing in an extensive list of primary sources, many originally published in French.

394 **Afrique Contemporaine.** (Contemporary Africa.)
Paris: La Documentation Française. 1962- . quarterly.
One of the major research sources for French-language material on Africa, this quarterly includes articles on current political, economic and social topics, a chronology of events in each country, capsule reviews of the most important literature published during the quarter, and a few biographies of African and French leaders involved with Africa.

395 **Annuaire statistique du Burkina Faso.** (Statistical annual of Burkina Faso.)
Ouagadougou: Institut National de la Statistique et de la Démographie. 1984- . annual.
A massive all-inclusive reference work, composed mostly of statistics, and ranging from climatology to the size of the civil service.

110

396  **Bibliographie des travaux en langue française sur l'Afrique au Sud du Sahara.** (Bibliography of French-language works on sub-Saharan Africa)
Zofia Yaranga.  Paris: Centre d'Etudes Africaines. 1984-  . bi-annual.
The best of several comprehensive bibliographies on sub-Saharan Africa. Although the bibliography covers research appearing in all languages, the best coverage is on French-language publications. An equivalent annual publication is Hector Blackhurst, *African Bibliography* (Edinburgh: Edinburgh University Press. 1984-  . annual).

397  **Bibliographie générale de la Haute-Volta, 1956-1965.** (General bibliography of Upper Volta; 1956-1965.)
Françoise Izard, Michele d'Huart, Phillipe Bonnefond.  Paris: CNRS, 1967. 300p.
Comprehensive bibliography of primarily French-language publications on Upper Volta, a follow-up to the earlier work by Françoise Izard, Michele d'Huart, *Bibliographie générale de la Haute-Volta, 1926-1955* (Paris: CNRS, 1967. 246p.).

398  **Bibliographie nationale agricole burkinabe.** (National Burkinabe agricultural bibliography.)
Ouagadougou: Ministère de l'Agriculture et de l'Elevage, 1984. 44p.
Bibliography of material published on Burkina Faso's agriculture.

399  **Bibliographies for African Studies 1970-1986.**
Yvette Scheven.  London: Hans Zell, 1988. 637p.
A cumulative listing of 4,500 bibliographies published between 1970 and 1986.

400  **Burkina: statistiques économiques et monétaires.** (Burkina: economic and monetary statistics.)
Dakar: Banque Centrale des Etats de l'Afrique de l'Ouest.
three-monthly.
Compendia of economic statistics organized into a variety of tables, published by the Central Bank of Francophone West Africa. Formerly *Haute-Volta: statistiques économiques et monétaires*, this is the most authoritative and most easily accessible reference source for Burkina Faso's imports and exports, prime suppliers and clients, money supply, production levels, salaries, consumer prices and other economic indicators. The Bank also issues other material, including a bibliography of official publications, which appears every three months for each country.

401  **Burkina Faso.**
In: *Africa South of the Sahara.*  London: Europa Publications
1971-  . annual.
This important annual provides a country-by-country survey of Africa. The sections on Burkina Faso usually encompass around seventeen pages, including a number of compact articles summarizing the country's physical and social geography, history, economy, and recent political evolution. The section concludes with statistical tables on all aspects of the country including a breakdown of its livestock and crop

production, imports and exports, and a 'Directory' that lists members of the government, diplomatic representatives, publishers, government regulatory bodies, banks and so on.

### 402 Burkina Faso.

In: *Africa Contemporary Record*, edited by Colin Legum. New York: Africana Publishing, 1966-1989. annual.

This invaluable reference work on Africa has unfortunately been discontinued. Comprising a country-by-country outline of the year's most important socio-economic and political developments, the Burkina Faso sections have consisted of around ten pages, concluding with statistical data. A second part of the hefty volume carried thematic essays of current importance for Africa as a whole.

### 403 Burkina Faso: A Country Report.

London: Economist Intelligence Unit. 1973- . quarterly.

A quarterly containing selective compact political and economic analysis, and economic forecasting for the future. The same publisher issues a 'Country Profile' for each country on an annual basis.

### 404 Eléments de bibliographie sur les pays du Sahel. (Elements for a bibliography of the Sahelian countries.)

Françoise Beudot. Paris: OCDE, 1986. 175p.

A periodically updated bibliography of the countries of the Sahel, including Burkina Faso.

### 405 French-speaking West Africa: Upper Volta today, 1960-1967.

African Bibliographic Center. Westport, Connecticut: Negro Universities Press, 1968. 37p.

A selected, briefly annotated bibliography for the period 1960-67. See also Julian W. Witherell, *French-speaking West Africa: a guide to official publications* (Washington, DC: Library of Congress, 1967. 201p.). In the latter the specific references to Upper Volta are found on pages 141-5.

### 406 Haute-Volta. (Upper Volta.)

In: *Répertoire des centres de documentation et bibliothèques.*
(Catalogue of documentation centres and libraries.) Abidjan: Conseil de l'Entente, Service de Documentation, 1980, p. 169-201.

Although dated, this is still a useful guide to the sources of documentation (covering banks, cultural centres, universities, libraries and other structures) in the Council of Entente states that include Burkina Faso. The guide is well organized and includes hours, access to libraries, publications issued, and other useful data.

### 407 Historical dictionary of Upper Volta.

Daniel Miles McFarland. Metuchen, New Jersey: Scarecrow Press, 1978. 217p. bibliog.

Part of a 45-volume series, this work, soon to be available in a revised second edition, is composed of a 52-page chronology for the years 700-1976; a 108-page dictionary of entries arranged alphabetically with capsule information on an array of personalities, groups, structures, and social, economic and political events; and a 52-page bibliography. For additional political biographies, especially for the 1960s and 1970s, see also *African biographies* (Bonn: Verlag Neue Gesellschaft, 1971. looseleaf); *Les élites africaines* (The African élites) (Paris: Ediafric, 1971. 328p.); *Personnalités publiques de l'Afrique de l'Ouest* (Public figures of West Africa) (Paris: Ediafric, 1968. 300p.); 'Upper Volta' in *The new Africans*, edited by S. Taylor (New York: Putnam, 1967, p. 472-83); John A. Wiseman, *Political leaders in Black Africa* (Aldershot, England: E. Elgar, 1991. 249p.).

408 **Inventaire des études, recherches et enquêtes menées sur le marché céréalier au Burkina Faso entre 1977 et 1988.** (Inventory of studies, research and enquiries into the cereal market in Burkina Faso between 1977 and 1988.)
Dramane Coulibaly, Daniel Martinet. Paris: OCDE, 1989. 103p.
Comprehensive bibliography of research conducted during the period 1977-88 on the marketing of cereals in Burkina Faso.

409 **Répertoire fichier des entreprises du Burkina Faso: 2e recensement industriel et commercial.** (File catalogue of Burkina Faso: second industrial and commercial inventory.)
Ouagadougou: Institut National de la Statistique et de la Démographie, 1988. 293p.
Greatly expanded from the first (1986) edition, this work is a province-by-province inventory of private, state and mixed enterprises in Burkina Faso. Extremely well presented in the form of individual entries for each entity, with comprehensive details on ownership, date set up, capitalization, official name, number of staff and director, the work concludes with an alphabetical index. See also *Analyse des résultats du recensement industriel et commercial* (An analysis of the results of the industrial and commercial inventory) (Ouagadougou: Institut National de la Statistique et de la Démographie, 1988. 88p.).

410 **Répertoire national des entreprises.** (National directory of enterprises.)
Ouagadougou: Chambre de Commerce, d'Industrie et d'Artisanat. 1986. 82p.
Directory of all commercial enterprises in Burkina Faso.

411 **République de Haute-Volta.** (Republic of Upper Volta.)
In: *Africa administration: directory of public life, administration and justice for the African states*, edited by Walter Z. Duic. New York: K. G. Saur, 1978. vol. 1, p. 489-550.
A unique, compact but detailed presentation of data on the country's administrative regions and capitals, towns, villages, city quarters, names of cabinet ministers, radio and TV stations, embassies, local government authorities, mayoral offices, international organizations, rural constabulary, gendarmeries, regional army commands, hospitals, airfields, financial authorities and banks, all with addresses and telephone numbers. The work also includes a list of all professional offices such as lawyers, engineers, doctors, and architects, as well as lists of all schools, sports clubs, hotels,

waterworks and electricity plants. Some of the information is dated, but not easily obtainable elsewhere. The material is organized for readers conversant with English, French, German, Dutch, Spanish, Italian and Serbo-Croat.

412 **Sociétés et fournisseurs d'Afrique Noire.** (Societies and suppliers of Black Africa.)
Paris: Ediafric. 1964-   . annual.
This trade directory of French Africa has been defunct since the late 1980s. Arranged alpabetically by country, the 'Haute-Volta' or 'Burkina Faso' section comprises around seventeen pages, providing capsule information on all private or mixed companies in the country, their address, telephone and fax numbers, capitalization, name of managing director, and equity share of the owners. In a separate section are listed all major European companies involved in trade with French Africa, with equivalent data about them.

**Atlas de la Haute-Volta.** (Atlas of Upper Volta.)
*See* item no. 1.

**Burkina Faso.**
*See* item no. 2.

**Burkina Faso.**
*See* item no. 3.

# Indexes

There follow three separate indexes: authors (including editors, compilers, contributors, translators and illustrators); titles of publications; and subjects. Title entries are italicized and refer either to the main titles or to other works cited in the annotations. The introductory definite or indefinite article is omitted from titles in English. The numbers refer to bibliographical entries, rather than page numbers. Individual index entries are arranged in alphabetical sequence.

## Index of Authors

117

119

# Index of Titles

## A

124

127

# Index of Subjects

129

# Map of Burkina Faso

This map shows the more important towns and other features.

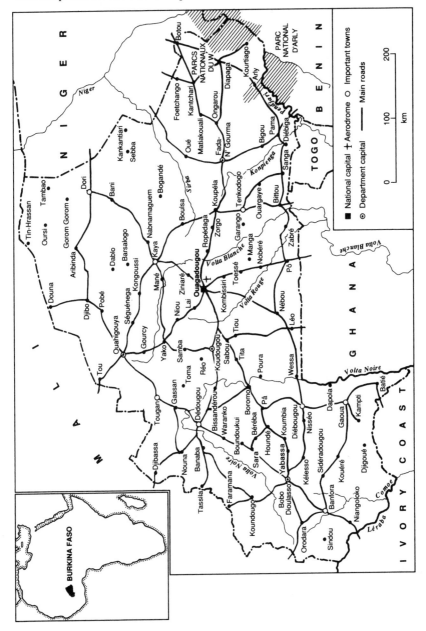

IRELAND'S LEGENDARY WOMEN

for Amy, my granddaughter,
and all the young girls of Ireland

Rosemarie Rowley

# IRELAND'S LEGENDARY WOMEN

ARLEN
HOUSE

*Ireland's Legendary Women*

is published in 2016 by
ARLEN HOUSE
42 Grange Abbey Road
Baldoyle
Dublin 13
Ireland
Phone/Fax: 353 86 8207617
Email: arlenhouse@gmail.com
arlenhouse.blogspot.com

Distributed internationally by
SYRACUSE UNIVERSITY PRESS
621 Skytop Road, Suite 110
Syracuse, NY 13244–5290
Phone: 315–443–5534/Fax: 315–443–5545
Email: supress@syr.edu

978–1–85132–156–8, paperback

Typesetting by Arlen House

Cover images by Jim Fitzpatrick:
'Diarmuid and Gráinne' and
'Derdriu and the Sons of Uisliu'
reproduced with the kind permission of the artist
www.jimfitzpatrick.com

# CONTENTS

# IRELAND'S LEGENDARY WOMEN

# THE WOOING OF ÉTAIN

1

i

Never such a shivering tale be told
Étain bathing by the stream one day
saw a horseman whose brooch and hair were gold
he was a man in beautiful array
his shield and buckle gold, his eyes were grey
his strap of silver and his five-pronged spear
gold as the barley at the turn of year.

ii

The rider told her of the fairy forts
was this prophecy, or was it dream
desecration of the fairy world imports
a nightmare of what we are or seem
and battle with kings who would deem
it honour to dispute her name
but peace within her beauty still reclaim.

iii

The maidens shied away from such a man
others made bold to hold his silver gaze
then Étain remembered heaven's plan
something that would haunt her all her days
the King's eye healed, another king to faze
the drowned horses and the Tethbae birds
she to be swallowed in the big Queen's curds.

iv

The hooves danced with the cutting of the blades
in tunic red and cloak of deepest green
he turned his back to Étain and her maids
heading back to lands as yet unseen
she would remember what such colours mean
borrowed from her the green eternal world
the red was rowan berry, death unfurled.

V

The High King thought she was his to woo.
And won her after a summer's night
her heart did not stir for him, as he who
rode in the memory like a vision of the light
the king possessed her, did not own her sight
nor touch, nor hearing, she was yet another's
whose mystery dwelt in the lives of others.

vi

He saw her unwind her plaited golden hair
loosening the golden braids with a silver comb
her tunic was red and green, each golden layer
like the year's turning, handsome as they come
as sweet as life crammed in a honeycomb
her arms, silken, slender, white
her head a silver circle in the night.

vii

Years later, when all that was left was talk
in Tara there was held a loving feast
at such momentous meeting lovers balk
but Eochu the King had his magic tryst
and sent out word the greatest was the least
Étain's famous beauty now enriched him
he had seen her bathing, it bewitched him.

2

i

The king's brother, Ailil, was stricken
the Druid said it was love or jealousy
so he pleaded with Étain that she quicken
his life, though he was vowed to celibacy
three times a date was set, three times fallacy
until stood before Étain her former prince,
her husband, Midhir, not forgotten since

ii

The day she saw him in the red and green
reminders of the holly and the berry
the scent of wild flowers to the eye unseen
the secret of the eternal in the merry
faultless land of the fairy queen
where she was, eternal, and he her mate
living in an unfallen, unblemished state.

iii

'I was once your husband in a fairy land
where there is no birth in sin or pain
only children born to a joyous band
with yellow hair, white skin and foxglove stain
not withering to age, but honeyed rain
sweet water, mead, making a pleasant drink
eternal life promised at the brink.

iv

My first wife, Fuaimneach, was a sorceress
with a red rowan wand she cast a spell
turned you into a pool of water, no less
than what was between us, to create hell
she then turned you into a worm as well
and as a scarlet butterfly you flew with me
in a wild tempest across the sea.

V

Your father's wife swallowed you in a drink
you were born on Earth and lost to me
how deep is Paradise, I can only think
it meant nothing when you weren't there to be
loved by your husband, you know I am he
come to reclaim you to your rightful place
in fairyland within a mythic race'.

## vi

The earth-husband, Eochu, had a visitor
a stranger clad in purple and in gold
with a chess game challenged the Inquisitor
let him win, five-fold and ten-fold
dark grey horses, broad-chested, with firm hold
wide-nostrilled, swift, dappled red ears
enamelled bridles for the fifty dears.

The next night there was wagered fifty boars
curly-haired, fiery, contained in a blackthorn vat
fifty white red-eared cows and calves without sores
fifty swords, gold-hilted, ivory blades to follow that
three-headed wethers, fifty cloaks. He spat
another wager to clear stones, lay a road
the fairy folk at night worked at such a load.

3

i

The final stake was a kiss from Eochu's queen
a month postponed, the hire of fighting men
but she had already dreamt the red and green
her husband had to give permission when
Midhir asked for a kiss and in that crafty ken
their lips met and when she opened her eyes
she was back in the fairy Paradise.

Eochu saw two swans with a golden chain
fly disappearing into the air
and in the fairy land, life renewed again
Étain was to give birth to his heir
on the first of May, the child was born, so fair
by Midhir's request, also called Étain
he didn't mind another's child to gain.

iii

By a silver stream mother and daughter dreamed
their life eternal, beautiful and kind
Étain the younger, wondered how life seemed
so dull, when tales of mortal mind
of feast and famine, light and dark combined
to her, an interesting, fascinating story
Tara in its golden Celtic glory.

iv

Eochu, at home, longed for his wife
he dug up mounds to find the fairy fort
each morning not a blade of grass or life
disturbed the rolling hills of Tara's court
while ravens came to stir anger, stayed to sport
blind dogs and cats stood guard with limping hounds
Scleth and Samhair, Eochu's anger knew no bounds.

v

Midhir came back to Tara, to ask
why he was persecuted by the king
'I do not consider you wooed fairly in the task
you who sought magic ways to bring
my wife Étain to the world of eternal ring'.
'I will by tomorrow Étain return
if you desist from deeds, my name to burn'.

vi

By the third hour on the morrow there were fifty
Étains in the mist surrounding the mound
an old hag whose age count was quite thrifty
stood before him without a single sound
which of them was his true love in the round?
He saw one with a genuine aura
who appeared to be a skilful pourer.

vii

That night, with Étain sleeping in his arms
he found love, remembering his youth
and he was quietened by her fairy charms
her freshness, with her show of ruth
till Midhir mocked him with the awful truth
confessing his joy to him across the water
learnt he had slept with his and the first Étain's daughter.

4

i

Such treachery broke the heart of the earthly king
he now looked at the young girl with pain
how he was saddened in this golden ring
had lost his soul his bitter heart to gain
sick at heart that he had with their daughter lain
she was now pregnant with his child
so he banished her forthwith to the wild.

ii

Étain the second was faced with the cruelty of the world
she who already had been to Paradise
now in the wild wood, with the king's anger hurled
at her beneath the stormy, earthly skies
she would have to grow old in pain, be wise
the infant to whom she would give birth
snatched from her, to be cradled in the earth.

iii

The men came and snatched away the child
a beautiful girl, with embroidered cloth
the name Étain thrice-born was now defiled
she was going to be destroyed through wrath
as the evening hour drew upon the moth
wondering which men were angels, which were weak
to smile on a little girl, not vengeance seek.

iv

Her mother, stricken, wept both night and day
mourning her daughter she never would see
she who was beautiful, was now bereft
of gladness, grace, of joy that could not be
a desert life as dry as dust, no glee
but mourning like the grey and bitter hag
who brought her to earth, the burden of a nag.

v

There were no more feasts at Tara, now deserted
the king died, his mind and heart oppressed
Étain searched the mounds, they were converted
against the Sidhe a borderland undressed
to which rough soil her silken face was pressed
and so to death, it seems for being a mother
the king her husband, to whom she was wife and daughter.

vi

Mind against mortal raged and won the day
death was a cup as bitter as the gall
when offered life, no one seemed to pay
the end foreclose, to live or not the pall
death had such sting, why do we live at all
only the fairy folk know the answer
to live forever as a golden dancer.

vii

Who can choose to be mortal or immortal?
A fairy love that can last forever
a threshold on this earth that has no portal
choosing can mean from those we love we sever
all healing love bands, as if ever
to the wildwoods ringing our departure
never signaled by the one-eyed archer.

5

i

With her tunic embroidered at the breast
young Étain was taken to the woods
the men stopped at Findlam's for a rest
resolved to go no further – the bud
where rested the green and red royal blood
to a guard-dog puppy she was given
to a humble cottager: at last forgiven.

Her existence brought a blessing on the couple
her beauty all over gained renown
her face was fair and full, her body supple
in beauty, she was given Nature's crown
and all who knew her loved her, not a frown
lived on her handsome forehead, but a glance
as she embroidered made hearts dance.

iii

The years went by, untroubled rural calm
the mortal parents were bursting with pride
the king forgot the child, the dreadful sham
and soon to mortal doors, which opened wide
and closed again, as he, his story died
but in people's hearts there remained a story
of Tara, of its blight and of its glory.

iv

Eterscél was a new king in the province
he heard of Étain's beauty, and resolved
to go and woo her, he would convince
her parents that with her was dissolved
all harm, all evil, problem to be solved
the world with love and wonder would not cease
there would be the beginning of a peace.

V

She had been brought up in isolation
now to learn the touch of human hand
a bird flew above in exaltation
rested his breast on hers in loving band
eyes closed, he stroked her as the land
whence she came, from dear earth as a child
would come the son of Eterscél, bound in *geasa*,* smiled.


* promises

vi

Born with three gifts, the greatest gifts to see
what could not be seen by any of sight
nor judgement, that brought good to be
but his father's sins were endless as the night
not to shoot birds, in Tara, around in flight
there was hope that harm in Étain be undone:
not a stranger be admitted to the dun.

vii

So Étain birthed a new hero who grew only to die
between times, carved out a noble life
loved and honoured, though neither could fly
back to the end of youth, the end of strife
Conara, son of Eterscél, with promise rife
broke *geasa*, his heroic antique vows
the night he was slain in the Three Reds lodging house.

# THE ENGAGEMENT OF EIMEAR

1

i

Cuchulainn's skills in the art of war
renowned in Emain Macha of old
made elect warriors think very far
that he should have progeny as bold
for he would not live long, it was foretold
too young, too brave, too beautiful
he should have a mate ere the year was full.

ii

Cuchulainn went to the garden of Lugh
to seek a mate, she would have the gifts
he met Eimear as he came upon the view
of beauty, voice, sweet words, wisdom, no rifts
but chaste needlework and such lifts
to the soul – yet with such security
he knew she was renowned for her purity.

iii

'May the gods make all roads smooth
before you', she said to her prospective man
'and may you keep from every harm, each booth
safe as the ladies now engaged in what can
be done in needlework, nor riddle ban'.
As they conversed in sweet talk
it seemed as if the gods did not run amok.

iv

'What a fair country in the bosom of your dress'
Eimear smiled her winning smile
'no man will travel these to caress
this sacred land until he kills with guile
a hundred at every ford or mile
between Scemen and Banchuin Arcait
a hundred men at every hit'.

V

'That is a resting place at the blossom of your gown'
'Thrice nine men with a single stroke, spare no one
drinking earthly blood as they fall down
it must be so if my heart be won
and the life spared on what the sun has shone
we will remember all at our wedding
where we can re-arrange the bedding'.

## vi

'That is a respite at the top of your dress'.

'None may travel there who is from Samhain asleep
to the lambing time at Imbolc, no less
without sleep again from Imbolc to Bealtaine or weep
and from Bealtaine to Lughnasa the fruit not reap
until it comes round, yields all fruit again
then I will consider you for your pain'.

vii

The maidens left whispering the strange words.
Eimear's father heard, disguised as a girl
a chieftain at whose banquet the birds
flew over as he praised them loudly, all
the feats of deeds by Cuchulainn would enthral
he would send him to the island of the Shadowy One
who would teach him tricks by which the world be won.

2

i

Eimear sadly watched her warrior leave
for the Isle of Shadows, on Scotia's misty coast
they swore to be true and not to grieve
that he would return to fulfil his boast
that he would scatter thousands in a host
he left having made his solemn vow
took Conchubar Laghair and Conall on the bow.

ii

Dornollla was a girl with a big fist
she sighted Cuchulainn and looked on him with lust
her hair was red and glowing in the mist
her face blackened with a sooty dust
she vowed to have him or alone he must
brave the shadow isle and the warrior queen
his companions deserted him, she was so mean.

iii

On the shores of Alba he now landed
a powerful beast then blocked his way
Cuchulainn tried to fight it single-handed
but it bounded up and down – made him pay
carrying him on its back day after day
on the fourth he came to the edge of a lake
threw him on the shore like a gavelled rake.

iv

The plain of ill fortune came into view
the blades of hungry grass made hairs perish
then a band of warriors, Scathach's crew
welcomed him to Scotia to cherish
their time in Ireland, not to nourish
and not to welcome, but here was a test
set by Scathach to find the best.

V

To cross a bridge that reared up from behind
he took an elegant salmon leap
in two gigantic strides, she was not blind
but welcomed him as pupil to her keep
but she had a hidden purpose very deep
Cuchulainn would sleep with Uachach's daughter
and find for her an heir to cross the water.

vi

Scathach gave her weapons to the hero
the enemy's scream, the cat's feat
balancing a spear and shield like a zero
the *gae bolga* to rip his entrails, defeat
all enemies, even Scathach's sister, greet
Aoife who tied him to a vow if he won
that she would bear him the gift of a son.

vii

Three wishes and the hero on his knees
his vows to Eimear were perplexity
but he vowed the warrior queen to please
take her niece in her complexity
for she had the gift of prophecy
would train him as a warrior second to none
spat on her hand: that night the deed was done.

3

i

A child fermented in a warrior's blood
to reveal his name to no one was his *geis*
or turn away a chance to have a flood
of combat where he might be as
fatally bound as Thermopylae to a pass
Cuchulainn left the shadowy isle
to return to Eimear, such was his guile.

ii

He hardly caught a glimpse that first year
Eimear still drew him with her skill
bright as she was with a crystal of a tear
sleepless he was and without a thought to kill
from the snows of Samhain to Imbolc's lambing, still
to Bealtaine and Lughnasa without a rest
he won each time through her need to test.

iii

He drew the chariot up to the fort
he saw her pride her hair at the window sill
thrice leapt the triple walls the salmon port
attacked eight of nine men, an easy kill
her brother spared according to his will
he rescued Eimear from her father's house
slew a hundred just to keep his vows.

iv

At each resting place he slew a hundred men
between ford and ford there was much slaughter
Forgall pursued Cuchulainn and when
he desisted he gave up his daughter
Eimear lost bitterness that he had crossed the water
gave herself and Emain Macha as wife
to forge honour, bring an end to strife.

V

Cuchulainn had left a thumb-ring for his son
in the Isle of Shadows Connla grew to stature
tried on each year it fitted, and he won
manhood in his seventh birthday, nature
drew him to a feast of nomenclature
across the waters he would seek his sire
but he was bound to promise very dire.

vi

To refuse to reveal to anyone his name
not to refuse ever to go into battle
or combat with a father soused in fame
who had fought for Ulster in the Cattle
Raid of Cooley, not to rattle
but take his destiny doing what he can
while a mere boy acting like a man.

vii

At Trách Eisi the Ulstermen were gathered
they saw the boy playing with the gulls
shooting and reviving them while men blathered
about likely high deeds with heroes and with bulls
or from their ancestral tales made many culls
all were agreed there was imminent danger
from this young boy who was not quite a stranger.

4

i

This is the augury of a dying day
chariot wheels never looked as bland
as the oil age has blown a future away
merciless under the sun and sand
all in a case of the scribe's hand
was Cuchulainn born with a caul
was he predestined not to see at all?

ii

Eimear herself had chosen a house, red
first colour that she loved, when she thought of blood
everything came to Ulster through her bed
she had in her father's love a radiant flood
to dip the centuries in to do no good
her marriage first be consummated in her head
until the whole warrior tribe was dead.

iii

'Who is kin to you?' she asked in honeyed tones
took a stole from the banquet of rags
'I like this severed from the usual ones
who prate at my door, if love creates such bones
my bones will rot before I give away
the biggest thrill to die on your wedding day
for which I have five thousand years to pay'.

iv

Two ceremonies in one, this bargain basement crap
Cuchulainn loved her flaunting of her breasts
the right breast is mine, the thumb ring my chap
she'll die in jealousy like a famine pest
envy a crust from the feastings done in jest
seven years I waited while we were cleft
his seven short summers on her left.

V

A fluttering of the beautiful mouth
that is the difference between life and death
in a moment passing all age and youth
speech stopped all in a breath
a shimmer and a sign, a wreath –
the same is killing a hundred, or one
no worse pain than killing your own.

vi

'Listen maidens', said Eimear to her cohort
'you all bedevil me to look like saints
when I have Cuchulainn for my consort
I'll let you all play with my pot of paints
I'll let you dye your clothes in scarlet report
of all the reds couldn't mingle till our bloods danced
he'll die on the gibbet for his heroic rants'.

vii

'Surely you will love him as your husband'
'not I', said Eimear, 'he will be my bridegroom
always approaching constancy like a riband
there is very little left to me of the moon
life and death, it's all over quite too soon
a vagrant witch only to come calling
I am impatient with this stalling'.

5

i

Condere was elected to go forth
persuade the boy to reveal his name
what connection he had with the north
would introduce him to the Hall of Fame
Ulster's poet, warrior, leader who came
to do his bidding at the mention of the word
otherwise he would be put to the sword.

ii

He made a few remarks about the sling
Conall then tried to chat with the warrior lad
he couldn't get him to change a thing
and the young stranger hurled a shot, bad
luck to him, Conall wounded on the forehead
the mystery around him grew
he had impressed so much the mighty few.

iii

Cuchulainn and Eimear were watching all the while
they were stunned with fear for the boy
he didn't show any sense or guile
but used his sling like a dreadful toy
who could such an upstart annoy?
Cuchulainn went to bring him out of anger
he who had been born of his own sweet languor.

iv

Eimear heard of the gold thumb ring
knew she had no equal in the nest
jealousy for her an only fling
for she believed she was the very best
and she could always take her queenly rest
yet Cuchulainn began to advance on the boy
whose own he was to create and to destroy.

V

He expressed to the boy his great admiration
he said he marvelled at the warrior game
for he had a certain fascination
and did not wish to really harm or maim
who was another him, almost the same
the boy looked with scorn about his father,
as if he'd anywhere else to be, rather.

vi

With one stroke of his childish mockery
the boy shaved the hair from his father's head
a father is the ultimate Comstockery
but bent on truths, the young boy led
wrestling his father off his mother's bed
ducked him three times into the water
his feet steeped in the stones of slaughter.

vii

The boy pulled his father down in the wave
Cuchulainn's reaction was quite furious
the *gae bolga* was a weapon against the brave
that he should use it on his son was highly curious
for it was famous for being injurious
his boy's bowels spilled along the sand
three days of mourning, slaughter throughout the land.

6

i

Eimear asking Cuchulainn on the engagement night
the girls had some partying in with the best man
it looked something on the lines of a conflict site
'did he penetrate your mind as well as your thigh?'
'I don't know' said Cuchulainn 'it was his constancy
all there was there, was lief to bring to an end
while he still had his reputation as my best friend'.

ii

'Reveal it to me, the secret of your friendship with Ferdia'.
'I never told him of my time with Scathach
she was my female self, my shadow
all I was then was to be a good fella
the time passed for my immemorial rock
whom I shall carry with me to my last breath
even to the pillory of my death'.

iii

'Is it then the Ravens who came calling
how they want to prise the secret from your body
your unblemished reputation your witless falling
your sacrifice to male bonding a threnody'.
'No one who knows me can doubt my autonomy
I reserve the best part for killing my son
the infamy will last as the ages run'.

iv

'I the Raven dip my bill in your blood
black is white and now it is red
black and white and red all withstood
now I pick at the waste of your bed
eyes now have a void, you have bled
covered the window in a black thing
because you liked the gleaming of my raven's wing'.

V

Like quicksand a polluted hurt flows
the blood of bloods exceeds all the rest
a gallant warrior whose hero further froze
when he beheld himself at seven years' pose
he killed his own, what the ancient knows,
his bones gave way to trembling like a blast
he had done the unforgivable at last.

vi

Only the wings of birds
beloved of the meddling gods
jealousy of the uplifting power of swords
how they covered the feasting bods
in their space where fire and sods
lit up the Arcadian darkness, as writ
sweet nuts, tender bed made in pits.

vii

Bed and death and bright nights down the earth
gave birth to a man, gave birth to a star
that encircles all the globe's girth
to tell the tale to make it travel far
a father who will kill his son, mar;
a strange inversion of reality
that now takes up our time with pity.

# THE SORROWS OF DEIRDRE

1

i

A right night for the getting of a child
or so it seemed to the poet seer
no matter that the wind howled loud and wild
this was an evening for forgetting fear
or so it seemed: nothing was so clear
to those who wanted mischief to beget
and put the whole of Ulster under threat.

ii

The prophet came to warn Conchubar the king
the child to be born would be to sorrow
beauty would be just a gift to bring
only strife and war, morrow after morrow;
beauty from time its precious fate to borrow
and it would cause much envy and despair
to all who looked upon such eyes and hair.

iii

Golden and glowing she would cause hearts to spin
passion to daze all who her beheld
the dazzling beauty, arms so white and thin
even the stoutest spirit would be quelled
and for her sake forests of men felled
for everyone who looked wanted to possess
more than a kiss, more than a golden tress.

iv

The harm done to Ulster would be great
such is the price of beauty undiminished
families bereft without a mate
young and old before their lives were finished
all for a glance in time that would be burnished
with tales of valour, treachery and spoil
all because such beauty is a foil.

V

A foil of surfaces that are nearly perfect
a mask, a covering of inclination
appearance was the key to every concept
beauty which had won such admiration
and gave to every man hope beyond his station
desire to turn to rue, regret and sorrow over
because beauty is the soul and heart's endeavour.

vi

Such is the price of Ulster's greatest heartache
the sight of perfection leads to killing
because beauty cannot be possessed to make
of anyone a hero that is willing
they must choose death if they felt such thrilling
bringing on their heads centuries of remorse
and in the clans a corpse upon a corpse.

vii

A seer well-practised to foretell
thought about Macha and her twins
the cruelty of forcing her to swell
then have the race where no one wins
least of all the Ulster men whose shins
tremble and waver like a woman giving birth
for centuries a blot upon the earth.

2

i

Then Conchubar the King spoke to the father
'I know a way I can spare you all this pain
let the child be and if you'd rather
I'll have her reared her precious heart to gain
and shield the province from the bloody rain
I have a nurse with whom she shall be reared
Labharcham her name, no good thing shall be spared'.

ii

And so it came to be, the child was born
Deirdre was her name and she grew
beautiful and lovely, none could scorn
the king's wish that she be reserved for the few
who could behold her and not be struck anew
by her extraordinary and flagrant beauty
the king could protest it was just his duty.

iii

The young girl grew in beauty and in grace
schooled by her nurse she was near perfection
a credit to her kingdom and her race
she blossomed under king's protection
she never dreamed that one day her rejection
of the king as her suitor would imperil
her life and freedom as a woman/girl.

iv

Few were the ones who caught a glimpse of her
most were afraid to appear in the bower
where her summering years were spent without care
save for the watering of a fragile flower
the odd raindrop from a passing shower
the tinge on her cheeks was like the dew
that promises each day to us anew.

V

Fifteen summers came and went, like dreams
she was tall and slender like the fresh-grown stem
but life never is as how it seems
her dress was often crumpled at the hem
and birds flew from her, she frightened them
there was something unruly in her gesture
that belied the sparkling innocence of vesture.

## vi

A sudden impulse would take all day to straighten
she often gazed beyond the wooden paling
perhaps it was hereditary as latent
as that which made her unpredictable when sailing
past the window with her skilled nailing
of butterflies to tapestries and needles:
she began to talk in urgent untaught riddles.

vii

The winter snow lay thick upon the ground
a bird came into view, a raven black,
she turned her gaze right and round
and said to nurse, 'this is what I lack,
a man who will not put me on the rack
with ugliness and age like King Conchubar'.
The nurse knew then that Deirdre was a goner.

3

i

The girl gazing from the window saw a berry
falling on the snow, it was bright red,
she suddenly became active and quite merry
and history records this is what she said
'the only man with whom I'd go to bed
would have hair like a raven, that bird –
skin as white as snow, red cheeks, that's my word'.

ii

Black, red and white, she then nailed
her colours to the mast and sat down sated
the nurse came by and loudly wailed
how on earth Deirdre would be mated
to a man they had not even calibrated
a handsome youth came suddenly in view
he was all Deirdre wanted, they both knew.

iii

She rushed to him and straight declared her love
she heard him singing such a tuneful song
she felt love rushing to her like a dove
the harmony didn't last too long
he broke off abruptly, felt it wrong
that he should intervene in her fate
she was the king's declared intended mate.

iv

Naoise said to Deirdre, turning her down
'you have the pick of men, our king
and your story is of such renown
I would not wish to meddle with everything
I am not in a position to give you a ring'.
She declared 'you make a solemn promise
that you can be mine for a caress'.

V

His honour was now under attack
he had to give her his word, or die
of shame, dishonour or hand her back
to her crafty nurse who couldn't tell a lie
he loved her so he couldn't say goodbye
so he swore then that she was ever his
and sealed the magic with a stolen kiss.

vi

The Ulster army heard the singing stop
and rushed to valiant battle for the girl
his brother Art and Ardal quick to cop
a situation was imminent, with peril
Conchubar called everyone in Ulster a base churl
who set off with the tragic pair
to seek in Ireland a chieftain's love and care.

vii

The seasons turned once more to winter cold
they camped out in the moor and the forest
ate wild herbs and killed for venison bold
and to each whose need was the sorest
at dawn the innocent birds chorused
that only humans hated one another
and all for love of the lady of their brother.

4

i

It is soon told: they had strong eloped
to Scotland where the beauty of its glens
gave substance to all they had hoped
the golden eagle and the sweetest wrens
not England with its cloud of vaporous fens
but Scotland with its mountains quite majestic
where they loved and slept and hunted all so hectic.

ii

The time grew long in pursuit of their game
soon they had outworn hospitality
and though for each other felt the same
they longed for the isle of serendipity
Ireland's saints and scholars, famed limpidity
of goodness, prowess, victory all in one
that lacked nothing but a constant sun.

iii

So they sailed back to Ireland all together
to face down King Conchubar and his men
but birds are seldom of one feather
and love when starved by beauty to all then
would come to a stop and a dark fen
symbolise the desirable and unattainable
they ran and ran, sat rarely down to table.

iv

The three brothers captured and were slain
Deirdre was soon taken to the king
he had done everything so her heart to gain
but broke here with an untarnishable ring
'you're mine now, I've got every thing'.
But Deirdre in pallor and remorse
was stricken with a grief of endless course.

V

She never smiled once in that given time
a year she grew morose and pale
she felt she had committed some dark crime
never laughed a laugh at dinner or with ale
she left everyone to tease or rail
furious Conchubar sent her to his brother
they took turns in staring at each other.

vi

They sat up in the chariot for a ride
she felt imprisoned by the men's bold gaze
each rode with her, side by side
gave her no freedom to look and talk her ways
her beauty which caused many to amaze
now was the warrant of her death
she dashed her head and drew her final breath.

vii

Her head hit the ground like a bouncing ball
the men looked sadly at what they had squandered
and thought if they hadn't asked for all
Deirdre might go where she might have wandered
found a mate as sweet as was her call
but now lay dead, a corpse all to behold
the story of her sorrows is soon told.

# TRANSLATIONS OF THE POEMS OF THE WOMEN BARDS OF CONNAUGHT

## DONAL ÓG

Donal Óg, don't let your words astray
but take me with you when you cross the water
you'll have a fairing on every market day
and you can sleep with the Greek king's daughter.

If you go without me I have your description
you have fair tresses and two green eyes
twelve yellow curls in your hair, a depiction
the colour of a cowslip or a garden rose.

It was late last night a dog barked where you stood
and the snipe squawked of your presence in the marsh
you were deep in solitude in the wood
may you be without a wife even if this sounds harsh.

You promised me and it was a lie
you'd wait for me at the sheep's paling
I whistled and called three hundred times my cry
and all I heard was a small lamb wailing.

You promised me something which came easy
a fleet of golden ships with silver masts
twelve townlands and the market busy
and a limestone court near the sea headfasts.

You promised me something quite impossible
that you would give me gloves made of fish-skin
that you would give me bird-skin shoes, incredible
and a suit of Irish material, the costliest, silken.

Donal Óg, I'd be better for you
than a haughty woman puffed with pride
I'd do your milking and churning for you
and however hard the blows, I'd be at your side.

Ochone, and it isn't that I'm famished
for the want of food or drink or sleep
it's the reason I'm skinny and almost vanished
my love for a young man has cut me deep.

It was early in the morning I saw a young man
upon a horse, taking the road
he didn't come near me nor exert a ban
on returning home, I cried a load.

When I go to the Well of Loneliness
I sit and cry till my heart's a stone
all life is around me, save a true caress
from him with amber shadow on his high cheekbone.

It was upon a Sunday I gave you my love
the very Sunday before Easter Day
I was reading the Passion on my knees, it behove
my two eyes sending you love all the way.

O mother, please let me have him, please
and give him all in the world I possess
even go out and beg for alms on your knees
don't prevaricate and deny me access.

My mother told me not to speak to you
today, tomorrow, or on the Sabbath
it was bad timing to be warned against you
The stable door closed: what's left is the ha'p'orth.

Black as the sloe is the heart inside of me
black as a lump of coal in a smithy's forge
black as a footprint in a shining hallway
as a dark mood overcoming humour's urge.

You took the East, and you took the West from me,
you took my future and my past, it's hell
you took the moon and you took the sun from me
and I greatly fear you have robbed me of God as well.

## FAIR-HAIRED DONNCHA

In this small townland happened a wonder
fair-haired Donncha hanging loose
the death cap on him his hat to sunder
his cravat replaced by a hempen noose.

I am approaching in the dead of night
like a helpless lamb under a flock of sheep
my breast covered and my head a fright
to see my dear brother in eternal sleep.

I keened the first bout at the head of the lake
and the second long scream at the foot of the gallows
the third agony at the start of the wake
in the midst of strangers, my mouth like aloes.

If I had you, where you used belong
down in Sligo, or the town of the Robe
I would break the gallows, cut the rope strong
and set fair-haired Donncha free from foreign probe.

Fair-haired Donncha, it's not the gallows you deserve
your place at the market and the threshing of corn
North and South, your plough would swerve
turning the deep red sod upwards to be reborn.

Fair-haired Donncha, sweet faithful little brother
I know the people who turned your life to blight
passing the goblet, reddening the pipe for each other
waist high in the dew in the depth of the night.

You, seed of Mulhaun, misfortunate harbinger of ill
he wasn't an amenable sucker, though you got him early
he was a fine figure of a young man, not yours to kill
who was made for sport and getting sweet sounds from a hurley.

O, fair-haired Donncha, is not death your spancel
in spurs and boots, no ornament would you worsen
I would put fashionable clothes on you, in your everlasting
    chancel
how I would deck you out as a noble person!

Seed of Mulhaun may your sons be scattered
may your daughters never a dowry seek
the two ends of your table empty and your floor splattered
for my brother you slew and his fine physique.

The dowry of fair-haired Donncha is coming home, you vandal
and there is no sign of a sheep, a cow or a horse
but tobacco, pipes, and a guttering candle
I won't upbraid them, to grudge would be worse.

It was at this time last year the mystery of my heart was absent
and he won't come back till he has perfected the ways of
    the world.
when I see him, I will run in a burst of energy to greet him,
to cover him with leaves, Jimmy my thousand darlings
    unfurled.

I'm getting continual abuse and roasting from my father
    and mother, it's savage,
I am torn into shreds, picked on, tormented and miserable
    in my life,
for I took a liking to the one with the fairest and most
    beautiful visage
and he went aboard ship, Jimmy with my thousand
    treasures rife.

I will go to the woods and there I will spend the rest of my days
in a place where there's no-one, as I listen to the birds sing
at the foot of the rowan tree, where there's grass in plenty
    always,
giving pleasure to Jimmy, my thousand times darling.

# IRELAND'S FAIRY QUEENS

## FAIREST OF THE FAIR
'Gile na Gile' by Egan O'Rahilly

Fairest of the fair, she was seen on the road alone
more translucent than crystal the green rims of her blue
   eyes bleak
yet sweeter than sweet the expression far from a wizened
   moan,
her tinge red and fair-hued, setting fire to the embers of
   her rosy cheek
there was a twist and a turn in every hair of her yellow tress
I saw the round perfection of the dew drop gathered like a
   glistening comb
like an accoutrement that was clearer than glass, on her
   swelling breast
springing to life a generation of hope in her creamy
   celestial home
give me the wisdom of the prophets and she so lonely in
   truth
the knowledge that he who is faithful will return and reverse
such information that the company was bewitched that
   forced him into sharp rout
and other sources I would not dream of putting into well-
   joined verse
such insipidity of impotence to let me weft into hard
   opinion, judge
I'd be a bondsman of slaves to tie me into hardship of truth
on the blue of the Blessed Mary I would seek protection
   from rashness lest I budge
from the story that the beautiful maiden vanished in flame
   in the breast of Luachra
I ran with the speed of the really volatile to pilot my
   nimble heart
through craggy borders and long-eared crests of trees with
   sallies by hand
through the darkness I came, not understanding how I
   found my part

of the way to the place of places magically put together by
    a Druidic band
I was beset by a hirsute drunken gang, thrown on a heap
and a mob of slender maidens with many a tight curl
cast me in irons without a wink of sleep
and a stocky brute took hold of her by the breasts – a churl
I told her in the highest expression of truth of which I was
    capable
that she had no right to be joined to so craven a lout at her
    side
when she had at all times a noble one who was able
and of three times over the finest of Scots blood, to make
    her his tender bride
when she heard my voice she complained with pride and
    round
the flood of tears coursed down her cheekbone
she sent me away out of the fairy mound
fairest of the fair, I beheld her on the road alone.
my trial, my trouble, my heartscald, my sorrow, my loss
our sunny bright darling loving and tender
tossed on the black horns of that twisted crew
there is no remedy till our Lions return over the sea and
    rescue her from such a bender!

KITTY DWYER

*Traditional: a code name for the cause of Irish freedom*

In the early to late evening and my flock secured from the
     slope,
in the bend of the leafy wood, my journey light-hearted,
     full of glee
the cuckoo, the blackbird and the thrush were in chorus
     with every true note
and at the beginning and end of each verse, the refrain
     that Ireland be free.

There is a little magic mound of green grass in the front of
     my house
and every sunny morning a fairy princess is sitting there
     before me
she has books of Irish, with a little bit of English through
     them,
and at the beginning and end of each verse the refrain
     that Ireland be free.

There are a thousand colours in her clothing and her shoes
     the colour of heather
and a dress of the new fashion on her of the kind a king's
     daughter would wear
and she said, 'Sit down, young man, for a little while and
     I will not delay,
but I tell you I'd be young again if Ireland would be free'.

She sat on the little bench beside me and my limbs hanging
     down
I thought she was not a mortal woman, that I was in
     danger beside her
'Are you Pallas, or are you Helen, or the first woman who
     fired my heart,
or the woman who ruined hundreds, who is related to
     Kitty Dwyer?'

'I am a woman in so much in pain since my partner went
    over the wave
my family are in slavery and weakened with no leap in
    their hearts of glee
but the clans of Ireland will rise up and every sword will
    be swiftly raised,
and it is the beginning and end of my story that Ireland
    may yet be free'.

# THE ELOPEMENT OF
# DIARMUID AND GRÁINNE

i

Gráinne heard that Fionn's wife had died
leader of the Fianna was left alone
now he would have no one at his side
he let out a low suffocating moan
he wanted a woman nailed to his breast bone
her father decided she would be Fionn's betrothed at a feast
unprepared, powerless, she was aghast.

ii

Gráinne spied a young warrior, Diarmuid
she loved his audacious beauty spot
none of the rest of his body was hid
and he had vowed with none a love-knot
nor yet with a woman child had begot
Gráinne thought fast: a sleep potion –
a recipe that had come beyond the ocean.

iii

All present at the feast were soon overcome,
Diarmuid alone was conscious and awake
there was nothing left for them but to dream
and Gráinne wanted Diarmuid for her sake's sake
a love story, a future together to make
Fionn looked older than her own father
she'd be with someone else, younger, rather.

iv

At first reluctant, he finally took the challenge
a sacred vow, a *geis* he was sworn under
as the party slumbered without their knowledge
Gráinne got Diarmuid to steal Fionn's thunder
and ran away with him, was it any wonder
that a young girl tried to make her own destiny
all accounts bear witness to their itinerary.

## V

Brave Gráinne and Diarmuid took to the woods
not sleeping or eating twice in the same spot
then there may have been many shoulds
but none is greater than the love knot
she girdled around Diarmuid while he was hot
they lay on rushes, graves, thistles, hay,
each bed was theirs one night, then away.

## vi

Their lovemaking, never rancorous, always honeyed
dewy youthful heads and limbs
it didn't matter that they weren't moneyed
but by day saw heaven's blue rims
far off the sea, where wonder always swims
people of Ireland were enamoured with their story
the memory of the chase, the lovers' glory.

vii

Fionn knew Diarmuid would be savaged by a boar
pretended to help, offered him water
his pride was rancid and very sore
and always he wished he had caught her
after all she was Cormac Mac Airt's daughter
the water slipped through his hands
until Oscar reminded him of warrior bonds.

viii

Diarmuid died of his wounds and thirst
Gráinne lamented they had so short a time
she knew he was her last and first
lover and willing partner in crime
they didn't need a history to rhyme
places in Ireland were named after their stay
the memory of their elopement never faded away.

# THE MOTHER

## The Lament of the Three Marys

O Peter, apostle, have you seen my radiant one?
My loss, and my sad loss
I saw him awhile in the midst of his foes
My agony, and my piercing agony

You two Marys, come close to me and mourn my bright love
My sorrow and my aching sorrow
What have we to mourn if not his bones?
My sadness, my enduring sadness

Who is that fine young man at the tree of the rood?
My despondency, my poor despondency
Is it that you didn't recognise your own son, mother?
My grief, my unbearable grief

Is that the infant son I bore for three seasons?
O my heartscald, my burning heartscald
The little boy who was born in a stable,
My desolation, my awful desolation

Is that the little son nourished in Mary's breast?
My sorrow, my unending sorrow
Hold your silence, little mother,
And don't be distressed

And is that the hammer that drove in the nails?
My fright, my ghastly fright
And is that the sword that slit his side,
My terror, my abounding terror.

And is that the crown of thorns on his lovely head?
My desolation, my devastation
Listen, mother, don't be agonised
My distress, and my sore distress.

Listen, dear mother, and don't be sorrowful
My longing, my dreadful longing
There are women who will lament that are not yet born
My hurt, my profound hurt

There is no one whom you will mourn in the garden of
    paradise
My agony, and my grief,
What a bright rest you will have in the heaven of grace,
My pain, and my abiding pain.

Acknowledgements are due to the editors of *Books Ireland* and the *Cork Literary Review*, to the producers of BBC's Woman's Hour, to Sheila O'Hagan, and to the editors of *Transverse*, the publication of the University of Toronto's Comparative Literature Department.

My thanks to Alan Hayes, publisher at Arlen House, for his dedication and diligence and care.

Thanks are due to Professor Maurice Harmon for reading and commenting on this work and to Margaret Burns for proof-reading.

ABOUT THE AUTHOR

Rosemarie Rowley, born in Dublin in 1942, has written extensively in form, including terza rima, rhyme royal and rhyming couplets. She is a four times winner of the Epic Award in the Scottish International Open Poetry Competition. She has degrees in Irish and English Literature, and philosophy from Trinity College Dublin, an M.Litt on the nature poet Patrick Kavanagh, and a diploma in psychology from the National University of Ireland. She has been active in the green movement in Ireland and in the Irish Byron Society and worked for a time in the European institutions in Europe. She has given papers for academic conferences in Ireland, the UK, the USA and several universities on the European mainland.

Also by Rosemarie Rowley:

*The Broken Pledge* (Dublin, Martello Press, 1985)
*Freedom and Censorship: Why Not Have Both?* (Rowan Tree Press, 1986)
*The Sea of Affliction* (Dublin, Comark, Rowan Tree Press, 1987)
*Politry* (Dublin, Rowan Tree Press, 1988)
*Flight into Reality* (Rowan Tree Press, 1989)
*Hot Cinquefoil Star* (Rowan Tree Press, 2002)
*In Memory of Her* (Rowan Tree Press, 2008)
*Girls of the Globe* (Arlen House, 2015)

www.rosemarierowley.ie